The Great Pause

Blessings & Wisdom from COVID-19

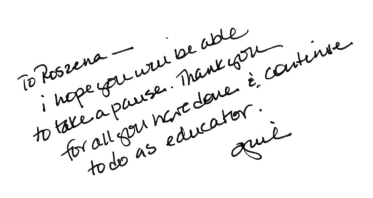

To Roszena —
i hope you will be able
to take a pause. Thank you
for all you have done & continue
to do as educator.
que

Elizabeth B. Hill, MSW with

Karla Archambeault, Jacqueline A. Baldwin, April Goff Brown, Anne Collin,
Ian Charlery, Dr. Christine Rapp Dombrowski, Michael Robert Eck,
Stephen Fowler, Elizabeth Hall, Ryan D. Hall, Davidson Hang,
Michele Kean, Brittany Luna, Dr. Barbara E. Milton, Jr., Christine A. Mola,
Melissa Molinero, Caren Pauling, Gina Raposa Johnson,
Dr. Davia H. Shepherd, Denise M. Simpson, Kristi H. Sullivan,
Kathleen Troy, Mary Ann Waterman, and Annamarie Wellington

GREEN HEART LIVING PRESS

The Great Pause
Blessings & Wisdom from COVID-19

ISBN (paperback): 978-0-9991976-5-3
ISBN (ebook): 978-0-9991976-4-6

DEDICATION

for those that have laid down their lives
in order for the world to
come home

TABLE OF CONTENTS

Elevation

normal

bird's eye view

transformation

Dear Reader,

Get cozy. We have a story to tell.

It is a story of a time when we awoke from a great slumber.

At first it felt so odd, like we were in an alternate reality, or lost in a dream.

We grieved over the 'normal' we had lost.

We chose if we would sit in the quiet and listen to our hearts.

We chose how much we'd notice.

As I write, it still feels like I am in a dream within a dream. A pause within a pause.

And yet...it is really just the early morning. It is just the early moments of waking up.

These writers have chosen to face the voices in their hearts and heads. They have chosen to share these with you.

As we read, we get to decide if we stay awake or return to slumber. We get to decide what we accept as 'normal.' We get to decide what things we will pick back up. We get to decide what we'll tolerate for ourselves, for our neighbors, and our planet. What will we choose?

Blessings & Wisdom,

Elizabeth

Introduction

Why We Write

Elizabeth B. Hill, MSW

I was coaching more than thirty people at the time COVID-19 began. Many lived with anxiety as well as complex physical health problems. They were from all over the country (at least 15 different states) and from all walks of life. They were all the colors of the rainbow in terms of skin color, sexual orientation, politics, and religion. I had a guy who had eight rolls of toilet paper in each of his four bathrooms. He and his family were ready! I had a 90-year-old woman who lived by herself whose family was trying to convince her to move up to live with them and she wouldn't have it. She was still walking up to the post office by herself, thank you very much.

I heard some people long for the time when 'things would get back to normal.' Every time I heard that phrase, I felt myself cringe. With my background in social work, I knew what we considered 'normal' wasn't working for the vast majority of people. And it wasn't working for our earth. I wasn't sure I wanted to go back to that.

I began to feel I was being given this bird's eye view of our country for a reason. I was being given a glimpse into how 'normal' was failing us and that this wildly disruptive "great pause" was causing something very unexpected.

As I sat still and listened, this is what I found:

Everyone was experiencing something different.

Everyone was being given a different message.

Everyone was being given a gift.

And those that could come home and be present with it, could see it as such.

They could see the blessing that it was, even in the midst of heartbreak, fear, and confusion.

If they were courageous enough to sit with the heartbreak, sit with the fear, sit with the confusion, the blessing would appear.

I began wondering what other messages and blessings people were experiencing during this time.

I desired to know.

As she does, the universe was listening. The universe is always with us, if we only keep our eyes, ears, and hearts open.

One day, as if I was unwrapping a present, the idea of doing a book compilation on this theme came to me. It showed up in three completely different conversations with three different people in the same day.

It was a pause within a pause. And on this day, I happened to be paying attention.

The hair on my arms began to stand up.

I posted on Facebook the following questions:
1) Why is COVID-19 happening to us / for us?
2) What opportunities and blessings has it given us?
3) What do we dare to dream of for our future?

I invited people who would be interested in collaborating on a book on this subject to contact me. The response was swift and passionate. I could see this was a book that must be written and it was my job to pull it together. It didn't matter what else was going on in my life, this was coming to be.

Within a week I had over twenty-five contributors wanting to participate. Within a few weeks, our authors were selected, and they began writing their chapters-all while the situation unfolded in real time in their homes and lives, even as it continues now.

So here you have it. Twenty-five lived experiences. From Manhattan to San Diego, the Cayman Islands to France, Connecticut to New Jersey. Doctors, coaches, teachers, business owners, social workers, massage therapists, healers, food delivery workers, financial advisors, caregivers, parents, and grandparents. Women, men. Black, Asian, Latina, White. Gay, straight, and a few colorful rainbows in between. Religious and not. People whose work changed drastically and those whose work continued rather seamlessly. People living alone and in houses full of people. All were unearthing an ever-deeper journey into Spirit and meaning.

The collective is yearning for an understanding of why COVID-19 is happening. We yearn for a message of hope in the midst of this radical change. We seek a path forward into an uncertain future. This book focuses on what COVID-19 has done *for* us, not *to* us. It highlights the blessings and wisdom of this time, some hard-won. As you read, I encourage you to unearth and share your own blessings and wisdom. Our earth needs us sharing our stories. And so we shall.

CHAPTER 1

Raising Our Vibration: Transformation 2020

DR. DAVIA H. SHEPHERD

For as long as I can remember, since I was very young, I have always been carrying on a conversation. Back then I never felt any need to define it, but I know now that I was just in conversation with my higher self. Some of you might think of it as an imaginary friend. Some of you may think it's just plain weird. Some of you might be freaked out by me talking about this. And you wouldn't be wrong to feel that way, because, well, we've all seen the thrillers and movies, right? This doesn't usually have a happy ending. Well, my parents felt the same way.

I was always guided as a child, sort of like a sixth sense. To me that was perfectly normal. It was all I had ever known, but I can totally understand why my extremely religious mother and my uber-scientific father would find this absolutely disconcerting and why I was encouraged to bury this as deep within myself as possible. I mean, having a child who always says things like: "I had a feeling that would happen," or who might gently warn of a minor mishap before it actually shows up, or who might predict an unexpected visitor or boon... Like I said, we've all seen that movie!

There was one person in my life who wasn't taken aback by all this: my grandmother. Amazing woman! She would smile knowingly and say, "Oh, stuff like that happens to me all the time." No explanations, no judgment, just loving acceptance and all the fun that grandmothers are known around the world for. That's what she was about.

I ended up following in my dad's footsteps and heading in the direction of science and research. I wasn't even truly interested in patient care back then. I'm a recovering researcher: facts, studies, figures, bio-statistical analysis. That was my jam! No space in that picture for the little girl who held her mom's hand and pulled her back because she sensed a window was going to break. Couldn't explain that with science so it was no longer real to me and, after a while, my inner voice became very, very, *very* quiet.

It took a lot of living, ignoring my inner guidance, many rough times and life experiences that may be considered less than ideal, for me to start again searching for answers. My inner voice was never silenced entirely. During my darkest moments, in times of what we might call a crisis, I've experienced the greatest guided shifts. Those moments taught me that I am always supported, never alone. Would you believe that in my search, reading all the books, studying with the coaches and mentors and gurus, that I finally came full circle? One of my dear friends and mentors, Darla, reminded me, "Believe yourself." Now I know!

My inner knowing was never something for me to fear, never something to push aside just because it was unscientific. I was just born into the world, as we all are, with a guidance system, a direct connection to our higher power. I just happened to have enough of a quiet mind as a child to be more in tune with it than some of the adults around me, who may have forgotten who they truly are.

Most people know me as that doctor who talks about helping patients live healthier and happier lives. I get good results with patients. And I'm finally embracing all the parts of me that make me whole and I'm coming out - so to speak.

So yes, y'all. I'm easing back into becoming once again in tune with my intuition.

I have been hosting a women's group called Ladies Power Lunch (LPL) for the past seven years. Every year for the past few years, we have had a theme.

Over the past few years I've had intuitive hits about themes for the year. For 2019, for example, I was instructed by Divine Beloved to uplevel my business. Based on that instruction, "Uplevel" was the theme for LPL for the year 2019. LPL members wrote books, started blogs and podcasts, started doing more speaking engagements, basically anything that could take our business to the "Next Level."

Approaching the end of 2019, I received very strong inspiration in meditation that 2020 was going to be a year of great transformation. I remember pulling an oracle card that warned of a "storm brewing."

Since I was a kid until now, my guidance has always been right, maddeningly so sometimes. For those of you who have a strong gut sense and sometimes ignore your gut to your detriment, you know what I'm talking about.

Come 2020 it was clear as day to me that this year was going to provide an opportunity for and involve great shifts for all of us. We dubbed 2020 "The Year of Transformation," and even titled our LPL Spring Conference: "Transformation 2020." Couldn't have been more clear than that, because the day of our conference was the beginning of our local COVID-19 quarantine, and we ended up hosting it as a virtual event.

My New Year's resolution for 2020 was to not let my circumstances dictate my feelings and the energy that I put out into the world. Not letting the pictures of my life be the reason I feel how I feel. I asked Divine Beloved to help me to truly solidify this for 2020. They say be careful what you ask for. All I can say is, "Well-played, Universe!" I've had an opportunity to practice this every day in 2020.

All that has been happening this year and all that is coming, I have been looking at through the lens of transformation, both for the world that we are living in and for me personally.

Principles to Live By

I have a lot of opinions, but I only have two principles that I live by.

1. We can live our optimal lives. That means we can live longer, healthier, and happier. We can have amazing health, careers, work, lives, finances, and relationships - and we don't have to compromise in any area! We can have it all. We get to choose how we look at things and how we feel, what energy we are emitting and as we emit higher vibration thoughts, the world around us, our microcosm, and the world around us at large, with our little ripple contribution... the world changes.

2. The power of the collective is greater than the sum of her parts. When it comes to "the other," my one rule is support each other. It's kind of like the golden rule, but putting it into action. The question I'm constantly asking myself is, "Everything that I am doing, is it supportive of the other?" When we come together, oh, the things that we can achieve!

With all that has been ongoing with COVID-19, racial unrest, murder hornets, floods, and all the other plagues that we have been facing in the last months, it's easy to devolve into panic, fear, or we could look for the opportunity.

I am not encouraging us to put a happy face sticker on a bad situation. I am saying let's see the situation for what it is and then raise our collective vibrations to hope and positive expectation so that together we can carve something great out of what seems like a garbage sitch. You've watched HGTV and all the Do-It-Yourself home remodeling shows? I was addicted to them for a while. I think the attraction was how they could take a DUMP and make it into a palace! Trash and turn it into treasure. Do we have an opportunity here too? I think we do, and the outcome of all this is up to us.

Opportunities for Growth and Renewal

For a while I stopped watching the news. I heard about murder hornets and weather anomalies in brief. I meditated, went to work, came home, played with my kids, and started all over again the next day.

Then the race stuff started being in the news. I saw one report, and then another, and then another... and here's the thing I thought to myself: interesting. This stuff happens to black people every day. Sorry about these people, so sorry, and also nice that it's making the news, nice that it is being recognized, maybe something will be done about it.

Watching those news reports brought back so many bad memories, like the day back when I was pregnant a few years ago, and jogging in my community when I was stopped by a police officer who told me that a white neighbor had called and complained about a black woman on her street. He followed me with his car back to my home and advised me not to jog in my neighborhood in the future. When I recount this story to my white friends, they become outraged, but for me that was just a Tuesday...

Well, they say every new beginning comes from some other beginning's end. Maybe we can manage to keep this in the news cycle for more than the usual fourteen days plus or minus? Maybe we can truly usher in a new era of justice for ALL...?

I'm not trying to change minds. That's not my job. My job is singular. It is to speak my truth.

And here is my truth: Black lives matter, y'all.

And even as I say that, I can hear the response like an echo... the shouts of "All Lives Matter!" And, yes, every life is precious. But when I say my life matters, it doesn't mean that I think anyone else's doesn't. It's me reaching out for support. It's me saying to you, "Help me!"

I'm being treated like I don't matter. My parents and grandparents and their parents have been systematically and statistically treated like they don't matter more so than any other group every single day. I truly don't even care anymore about what society does to me, but it's my little beautiful babies that are growing up in this world that I cry for. That's why I say, "My life matters, their lives matter, help me help them live a better life." We are all in this together. It brings me back to my second life theme: the power of the collective is greater than the sum of her parts.

I want to say that for those of you who have suffered loss of any kind during this time, that our hearts go out to you. We too, both myself and those closest to me, have suffered tremendous loss during this time. We feel you.

That being said, what if...

What if this is the true transformation? What if this is the opportunity for us all to pause and go within? What if this is our time to really step into our greatness? Oprah and Dr. Nelson Mandela both say that *everyone* is capable of greatness. *Everyone*. What if this is the time to be in service, not in a self sacrificing way, not necessarily in a success-focused way, but in a way that serves the greater good?

What if this is the time for us to focus on what connects us even as we are being advised to remain at least six feet apart? What if, this is our opportunity to reach out to each other, with absolutely no expectation, no competition, and no agendas and watch what grows from that?

These images came up for me recently in meditation.

A Bright Light: We are in a time when we have access to increased clarity. We may be called upon in this time to be a guide for those who invite us. We are light workers and this is not a drill. It's time to shine our light.

A Stone: Representing the divine and eternal. Encouraging us to lean into our strength, the energy of the earth, to know that we have within us the capacity for endurance and that we access the best of our lives through appreciation.

A Web: We are all connected. All our lives have complex interconnections that we cannot even begin to imagine. Like the spider, we have the ability to construct the life we want to live. We have the capacity for incredible creativity. We need to let go of the traditional ideas of vulnerability and realize that sharing from our true selves, as Dr. Brené Brown teaches, makes us invulnerable. Our superpowers present themselves when we embrace and appreciate the power of our VOICE, the power of our words, the power of our communication, and the power of the connections in the collective.

I'm convinced that everything is influenced by the vibration that we are putting out into the world. What if more of us use this time of upheaval and uncertainty to raise our vibrations? The energy we are bringing to this will determine what our outcomes are. Abraham Hicks teaches, "one in alignment is more powerful than a million who are not." And so when I encourage you to rise up, this is not a call to arms, this is a call to raise our vibrations and create our world in the image we want it to be.

Selah.

About Davia

Davia is a holistic physician and master connector. A certified retreat leader and recovering researcher, she is celebrating almost 20 years in various areas of healthcare. She loves public speaking, is an international speaker, and bestselling author. She helps female entrepreneurs live the best version of their lives in every area: Health, Business, Relationships, Finances. She leads transformational retreats, conferences, and free monthly Ladies' Power Lunch events. Davia lives in the suburbs in Connecticut with her outstanding husband Wayne, two amazing miracle boys Preston and Christian, and her mom Phyllis.

"This is a call to raise our vibrations and create our world in the image we want it to be."

Dr. Davia H. Shepherd

Connecticut, United States

Breathe Deep

breath

chaos

courage

voice

CHAPTER 2

The Necessity of Breath: Adapting to Life in the Midst of a Pandemic

DR. BARBARA E. MILTON, JR., LCSW

*"Sitting here in limbo but it won't be long.
I know my faith will lead me on."*
-Jimmy Cliff-

America is on fire. It is imploding along racial, economic, and political fault lines. Our economy is in free fall at levels not experienced since the 1929 depression; civil unrest to protest police brutality is unlike anything we have seen since the 1960's and a coronavirus pandemic that could rival the Great Influenza of 1918 are all simultaneously occurring while there is a battle for the soul of our nation in the upcoming presidential election. The embers of fear and uncertainty swirl around us. We are all exposed to their toxicity. We are all breathing them in.

Cell phone videos capture the senseless and reckless use of force on black bodies by police officers. "I can't breathe" has become the mantra for a liberation movement as activists on the streets and in the halls of power press for systemic reforms of policing in our nation. They are not anti-police but anti-police brutality. I am a black life and I matter. I don't matter more than any other human being, just the same as every other.

"I can't breathe" is a state of being I can identify with from my earliest memories. I was born prematurely to a teenage mother. I was a blue baby because I didn't have enough oxygen in my blood and spent the first period of my life outside of my mother's womb in an incubator. I could not breathe.

Like generations of blacks in my family before me, I was groomed early on to work twice as hard as my white peers in order to succeed in school and life. I became the queen of dizzying doing in my social life, education and work. I had lots of successes. I had failures too. I was on the grind and hustling and having little time to catch my breath.

My wife, an avid gardener, used to ask me if I noticed the flowers she had planted. That was my one job, to notice her flowers. Rarely was I able to say, 'yes, I stopped and noticed the flowers.' My attention and focus was always somewhere else. I was always running here and there, if not physically, surely in my mind. There wasn't a moment to just breathe.

The first time I hit a wall that forced me to slow down and examine my life was the day I learned I had bladder cancer. That was on July 23, 2012. One week before, I peed in the toilet and when I turned to flush saw that the bowl was filled with blood. I gasped for air. I told my wife. I called my doctor. I had a scan. There were tumors. I had a surgery and the tumors were removed. I held my breath for several days and then I learned the diagnosis-urothelial carcinoma. This is a chronic form of cancer that I still live with and manage today.

Every ninety days I get scoped, the doctor removes the cancer, I receive treatment and then I live life until the next scope and surgery. It's a rhythm of life that my wife and I now accept. In 2016, the cancer moved from my bladder into my right kidney. At this point, the combination of my cancer, disc degeneration and worsening mental health forced me to separate from the workforce and the social work profession that I loved. I went on permanent disability. I needed to create space for some intentional healing in my life. I began to adopt ways to stop compulsive overeating, reduce anxiety and to tap into more spiritual practice aimed at recovery of my health.

So when the world went on lockdown for the pandemic I was already ahead of the game. I was on the path to better coping with stressors in my life. This coping grew from the use of many tools, the most powerful being my connection to something greater than myself. I call that God. I call that Love. I now connect daily to the source when I meditate and pray. I have slowed down. The practice of mindfulness in meditation at long last has taught me to breathe. For most of my life, I didn't know how to do that. My breaths were shallow and rapid; now I breathe more deeply, so much so that my belly moves in and out. Now connecting to that source of love helps me to have steady healing in my body, my emotions and my spirit. I am less reactive. I respond.

My breath is strengthened when I practice yoga and chanting. I do chair yoga with YouTube videos. I chant the daimoku buddhista chant - *Nam Myoho Renge Kyo*. I sing the sanskit mantra- *Sa Ta Na Ma Ra Ma Da Sa Sa Say So Hung*. I take the instruction of Thich Nhat Hanh to *"breathe in calm, breathe out smile, breathe in the present moment, breathe out a wonderful moment."* I am better able to *relax and take it easy* as I surrender to this practice one day at a time.

This breath makes way for love. When I am sending healing love to myself then I am better able pass it on to others. The world needs love to counter the hate and injustice that is entwined in the pandemic. Loving this way is radical and revolutionary. When loving-kindness reigns we can create a world of peace, justice, and equality. Only acts of love can make that happen.

It is a blessing to breathe. I am more fully alive. Life is different during this time of the great pause and requires adaptation. I miss hugging my grandchildren and my family instead we play game pigeon and FaceTime. I miss hosting and attending gatherings of my friends. Instead we have a regular Friday Happy Hour on Facebook Messenger.

I miss theatre and concerts. Instead many artists gift us their genius on various websites and media platforms. They know their art is a necessary balm during this time. I miss conferences and face-to-face fellowship-instead we Zoom. I miss traveling but I have figured out a way to scratch that itch by using a virtual reality headset. Most days I am whisked away to a beach on Maui, or hang out with animals on the Serengeti, or I am center stage with a jazz band in New Orleans, or on a challenging golf course practicing my putting. I am satisfied by these virtual experiences until we are safe and free to have them again in the real world.

The world has changed and so have I. I have slowed down. I am healing from grief, cancer, and compulsive behaviors. I am more grateful. I am more mindful. I am more woke and more hopeful.

My daily spiritual practice has enabled me to move through the grief of losing my beloved mother in January 2019. I miss Barbara E. Milton, Sr. every day of my life. Breath brought me and my mother forgiveness and healing. It helped me transform my grief journals about caregiving and my mother's journey through Alzheimer's Dementia into a book. The breath transformed our pain into a love story.

My daily spiritual practice helps me counter the anxiety and uncertainty of living with cancer. The breath helped me safely navigate New Jersey clinics and a New York Cancer hospital for treatment and surgeries during the height of the pandemic, during the time of mandatory stay at home orders and a ban on loved ones accompanying patients to medical services.

My daily spiritual practice helps me to be in a heightened state of gratitude. I am grateful I wake up each day. I am grateful my only kidney is still in my body. I am grateful for my health insurance and Social Security. I am grateful for all of my healthcare providers. I am grateful to be able to help others and do service. I am grateful there is resistance to injustice. I am grateful for the love of my wife, family and friends.

My daily spiritual practice has helped me to be more in the moment, even the scary moments of the awareness of my own suffering and the suffering of others, the pandemic, and civil unrest. Those moments have proven to be opportunities for me to grow more spiritual connection, more resilience and more activism. It has helped me tap into the power of love. Love for me. Love for others. Love for the world.

My daily spiritual practice helps me to use my breath in the service of working towards the dream of equality and justice for all. Dr. King said the arc of the moral universe is long but it bends towards justice. It doesn't bend by magic. I know that I have to do my part to bend the arc. The good news is that people all around the nation and the world are crying out for that change too. Love will conquer hate. We shall overcome. We shall have victory.

One day at a time I am becoming a better person, partner, friend, neighbor, and citizen. I pray. I meditate. I chant. I breathe. I write. And I kneel for all other human beings to breathe, too. Let it be so.

_H_ang
_O_n
_P_andemics
_E_nd.

ABOUT BARBARA

Dr. Barbara E. Milton, Jr. is a retired clinical social worker who for 40 years worked on behalf of at risk children and families and for the political enfranchisement of people on the margins of society. She is living with and surviving bladder cancer. She continues to be an educator, advocate and activist through her public access TV show, *The Dr. Milton Social Work Show* on Comcast in Northern New Jersey and through her YouTube channel and other social media platforms. She lives in New Jersey with her wife, Kay, where she is busy writing several books about her life, her beloved mother, her social work career and her research on inherited black resilience.

Website: www.drbarbaraemiltonjrlcsw.com

"The world needs love to counter the hate and injustice that is entwined in the pandemic. Loving this way is radical and revolutionary. When loving-kindness reigns we can create a world of peace, justice and equality. Only acts of love can make that happen."

DR. BARBARA E. MILTON, JR., LCSW

New Jersey, United States

CHAPTER 3

Chaos Creates Opportunity

MICHAEL ROBERT ECK

It has always been my belief that out of chaos, opportunity arises. The COVID-19 pandemic exemplifies this. Along with the global upheaval and crisis it has created, it has created opportunity. Opportunity to rise above. To find acceptance. To be of service. To be present. To renew faith. To adapt. To grow.

I first heard about coronavirus as I sat in a hospital bed at Jacobs Hospital in La Jolla, California, in January of 2020. This was my second go-around at Jacobs, the first stay due to my having contracting pneumonitis, a drug-induced—or, in this case, drugs-induced—pneumonia. The drugs, Opdivo/Yervoy, are a targeted combination immunotherapy developed specifically to treat metastatic melanoma, with which I'd been diagnosed three months earlier. This treatment, my team of doctors told me, was the therapy most likely to reduce or eliminate the malignant tumor under my arm. It was my best shot.

The treatment plan was that I would receive four infusions, one every three weeks. A week and a half after my first infusion, though, everything went sideways. Opdivo/Yervoy is a miracle drug for some cancer patients, but I experienced the very worst types of its side effects. Breathing became difficult, then more difficult. I began to cough up blood, then more blood, more frequently. Then I couldn't breathe without assistance, without oxygen. I spent the next twenty-six days in the hospital, the overwhelming majority of it in the intensive care unit (ICU), three of the days in an induced coma. When I woke up from the coma, my three grown daughters stood by my bedside: Jordan, 31, Kyrsten, 29 and Taylor, 27.

I had never felt so happy to be alive.

After spending Christmas and New Year's at Jacobs, I was finally discharged on January 6, 2020, sent home with steroids and a dozen oxygen tanks to repair my damaged lungs. My brother, David, and sister-in-law, Theresa, arrived the next day to help care for me. My lungs were healing and I felt my strength slowly return. A week later, as my brother and sister-in-law left to return home, Jordan and her daughters, my two granddaughters, Lily, 4, and Josie, 2, arrived from Connecticut.

I couldn't run around on the beach with Lily and Josie as I usually would, but I felt I was getting stronger each day. I was able, mostly, to move around and achieve my basic daily routines without hooking up to the oxygen tank. As the doctors had indicated that I would possibly breathe for the rest of my life only with the assistance of an oxygen tank, this was a huge accomplishment. Suddenly, though, my temperature skyrocketed to 104 degrees. I was having difficulty urinating. I assumed it was a symptom of Tafinlar/Mekinist, the new combination of chemo pills I was on, and was prepared to power through. Jordan, witnessing my difficulties late at night, wondered whether I might have a urinary tract infection, and suggested I call my oncologist.

The phone call likely saved my life. The on-call oncologist notified the emergency room to expect me, and from there, on January 20, 2020, I was readmitted to Jacobs Hospital. The diagnosis was sepsis and septicemia—an infection and poisoning of the blood—due to the sometimes harmful bacterium E. coli. On day two in the hospital, I was spitting up blood and having serious difficulty breathing again. The medical team put me back on oxygen and told me I might have to be intubated again. Why my lungs were struggling so severely again was a mystery, despite test after test to solve it. The answer soon revealed itself.

Watching the news that afternoon, I saw a segment on the coronavirus coming from China—that there were possible cases in the United States, most likely in Washington state. The coronavirus was killing thousands of people in China. Past that, information seemed sparse. An hour or so later, my nurse walked in. But something was different compared to every other time I'd seen her. She was covered from head to toe in "personal protective equipment," a term whose definition I'd soon learn.

"What's going on? What's up with the hazmat suit?" I asked.

"You've got coronavirus and they want us to be careful..." she answered.

I interrupted. "Wait, what are you talking about? I thought it was only in China—and maybe Washington?"

"Oh, no," she assured me. "It's not *that* kind. Coronavirus is actually a common cold strain that's been around forever."

"Okay...then, why all the precautions?" I wondered aloud.

"Just to be cautious..." she said.

In fact, a coronavirus—lower-case "c" and average, a common cold—had put me back in the hospital in dire straits. Its impact, layered onto the serious damage my lungs had undergone from pneumonitis, in a body combating cancer, had been extreme.

From there, briefly and as unlikely as it now seems, "coronavirus" became somewhat of a joke in my medical updates with friends and family. I'd just survived a plethora of potentially lethal complications while confronting an advanced cancer diagnosis. *Now I had coronavirus? How much worse could it get?* Of course, I didn't actually have what would become COVID-19, but whenever I mentioned my diagnosis of the common cold strain and used the term "coronavirus," people took a few steps back.

As the virus proliferated in the United States, whatever fun I'd had with my "coronavirus" routine of course ceased. The COVID-19 coronavirus, here, it was clear, was extremely serious. Everything became serious. In my own life, the impact of COVID-19 became serious, too. Surgery to remove my tumor had to be rescheduled twice: if San Diego experienced a spike in COVID-19 cases, rooms needed to be available for those patients; due to my lung damage resulting from pneumonitis, I was at additional risk to contract the virus in the hospital.

I was eager for the tumor to be removed. Putting it off increased the chances of the cancer metastasizing to my organs. I'd have to be on chemotherapy for a longer period of time. Overall, postponement sounded like a horrible idea. But "wishing" things were different wasn't going to help. Through a lot of prayer and meditation, and with an attitude of faith over fear, I accepted the fact that all would work out as most things do.

I was confident that spiritually, I had all the tools I needed, and I went to work. I connected with a healer specializing in breath work, meeting her daily on Zoom for two weeks leading up to my surgery. I prayed for perfect health. I meditated, visualizing the healing that was transforming my body. I stepped up my nutrition game with whole, healthy foods. I created a daily wellness tracker. I worked with a neuro-linguistic programming practitioner to remove any fear that may have been lingering from past experiences, most recently and notably being in the induced coma. I kept my body moving. I practiced yoga. I did different body weight exercises. I walked. I couldn't run much, but I did what I could. Being quarantined allowed me to be totally present and to fully engage in my healing journey.

On June 3, 2020, I was back at Jacobs Hospital, this time for just three days as my tumor was successfully removed. Interestingly, the three-month delay for my surgery, which I had first seen as an obstacle, proved beneficial. It gave my lungs more time to heal, and the chemo treatment and other healing work reduced the size of the tumor. I had "let go" of wishing for things to be otherwise, and, as is so often the case, it had helped things work out.

As a life coach, I consider myself a SuperHero Coach, my mission to help individuals tap into their power to live the heroic lives they were born for. *What does it mean to be a hero?* I believe it's heroic to live your best life, be of service in some capacity, and make the world a better place. During a period such as we are living through with COVID-19, no one needs a SuperHero Coach to bring out the best in themselves and others. Good always triumphs and millions of people around the world have shown this. My three daughters all represent examples of changing the world by doing some good in their immediate environments.

My youngest daughter, Taylor, is a fourth grade teacher at a magnet school in Wethersfield, Connecticut. When the state closed schools as a COVID-19 safety measure, many inner-city children were left unable to continue their education. They didn't have computers at home, didn't know how they'd get lunch every day—their parents didn't know how to deal with the unexpected cost or inconvenience of alternative daily daycare. Ms. Eck, as the kids call Taylor, was most likely the one constant force many of the children could count on. Day in, day out, Ms. Eck was there with a big smile, her passion to teach, and her willingness and ability to listen.

Although incredibly resilient, many of Taylor's students already live complicated and sometimes traumatic lives. With the added crisis of the pandemic, conditions and situations could possibly get much worse in their households. Like many teachers, Taylor had to digitally navigate the needs of each student in a way that was much more challenging than in-person interactions would allow. She spent much of her time listening to each child, ensuring that he or she had the opportunity to learn. The school district helped by providing internet services and computers to those that needed them.

One of Taylor's students is a lovely girl whose depression meant she struggled to get out of bed each day. Although the student was already meeting weekly with a social worker, what she needed was Ms. Eck. Taylor visited the young girl at her home, talking to her through a window. Crucially, she showed the child that she was loved and cared for by the one person she counted on every day.

My daughter Kyrsten works as a respiratory therapist at Yale New Haven Hospital in Connecticut. Only an hour from New York City, Yale was close to the epicenter of the COVID-19 crisis early on. As a top regional facility, Yale became the go-to hospital for the seriously ill population, which was comprised mostly of elderly and immuno-compromised patients. At one point, there were over 400 COVID-19 patients there, a large percentage of them in the ICU.

Kyrsten selflessly volunteered to work the ICU COVID floors, so that her co-workers with families at home could limit their exposure to the virus. She sent me photos in all her personal protective equipment—a phrase whose definition I was now fully familiar with—and shared some of her experiences. Working the overnight shift, Kyrsten was usually the only visitor for some patients, many intubated by Kyrsten herself. Because of safety precautions, visitors were not allowed, so she acted as an intermediary for patients and their families. On many occasions, Kyrsten incredibly had the courage to hold the hand of a dying patient as that person took his or her last breath.

Jordan, my eldest, is a business coach for a large insurance company. Like so many other parents of young children, she had to make huge daily life adjustments during this COVID-19 period. The wonderful day care facility that the girls had become accustomed to had shut down, requiring Jordan and her husband, Jesse, to create a game plan that worked for everyone.

They set goals. They drew up charts with checklists. They made schedules. As Jordan fulfilled the needs of her high-stress professional position, she juggled the responsibilities of parenting two curious, lively, growing children. Jordan and Jesse read wonderful books, took daily hikes and bike rides, made art, cooked meals, and engaged their daughters in other activities to build their smarts, imaginations, and capabilities. They seized a challenging situation and transformed it into a time for the whole family to be present and grow together, more connected than ever before.

Minutes before I was induced into a coma on December 15, 2019, I had called Taylor, who was in Connecticut getting ready to board a plane with Kyrsten. They were due to arrive in California late in the day, and as much as I tried to persuade the medical staff to postpone my intubation until they arrived, I failed. "It has to be done now," the doctors explained.

The reality of the situation, which the medical professionals made very clear, was that I might not wake up. Ever. While Jordan, who was already with me, teared up, I assured her I'd be fine. It was Taylor that would require the most reassurance. She was already in tears when she answered the phone, but I promised her the one thing I felt she needed most to hear. "Don't worry, I'll be fine, and I promise I won't miss your wedding."

This May 16, 2020, was Taylor's wedding day. With plenty of heartache, her purposefully and beautifully planned, large, farmhouse-style wedding had been cancelled a month prior due to Connecticut's COVID-19 precautionary health restrictions. Taylor and her fiancé, Ben, had decided to proceed with the marriage on that day, rescheduling the reception to June of 2021. The ceremony would include only immediate family: her mom and stepdad, sisters, brother-in-law, nieces, and Ben's parents and sister. The photographer they had hired for the wedding was there to capture the intimate ceremony.

Since I had promised Taylor I'd never miss her wedding, I planned to fly to Connecticut from California and walk her down the aisle with her stepdad. But that wasn't going to be possible. Because of my lung issues and ongoing battle with cancer, I was a high-risk candidate for COVID-19. I was, perhaps foolishly, ready and willing to take the risk and jump on the plane. I couldn't bear the idea of breaking my promise to Taylor, and the idea of missing her ceremony pained me deeply. Taylor, though, requested—insisted, eventually—that I not make the trip. It would add stress to an already stressful situation. "You promised you'd be around for my wedding Dad, and you are. I'm just happy you're alive, and we'll make the best of it."

At first, I was heartbroken. But then I thought about that fact that I'd survived quite an ordeal, and it was best to get into a state of gratitude, accept the situation, and celebrate Taylor and Ben's wedding the best way possible. Although three thousand miles away, the plan was to allow me the "first look" at the bride-to-be in her beautiful dress. Her sister, Jordan, called me via Facetime, and asked if I was ready to see my "little girl." I was ready. She turned the phone around to reveal Taylor, her hair and make-up in perfect order, stunning in her, indeed, beautiful dress. As our eyes locked, she brought her hand to her face in an attempt to control her tears. I did everything I could to fight back tears, as I was overwhelmed by both her beauty and the emotional roller coaster of arriving at this moment in time.

The moment—Jordan's hand holding the phone; Taylor, hand to face—was captured perfectly in a photograph. It is something I'll never forget. I can't imagine it being any more special had I been standing right there with her instead of three thousand miles away. I couldn't help but think of the thousands of potent emotional moments just like this occurring all across the country.

We all, human beings of every kind, have been altered by COVID-19. Like me, cancer patients have adapted and lived through its complexities and roadblocks. Children have adapted outside the schoolroom, continuing to learn from amazing teachers, who have had to abruptly and in some cases radically adjust the ways in which they teach. Vast numbers of medical professionals have adapted, working tirelessly in environments that often resemble war zones. Millions of parents have adapted, in many cases working from home while finding new ways to creatively raise their young children.

By accepting the things we couldn't change and changing what we could through service, we have stepped up to the task and lived heroically.

ABOUT MICHAEL

I am a SuperHero Life Coach. I consult with and help individuals, organizations, and community and corporate groups uncover and reclaim power in order to achieve their own meaningful objectives, and to lead their personally particular, authentic, heroic lives. I work with a wide range of clients moving towards all iterations of their own heroism. A cancer survivor with addiction recovery experience, and a martial arts and fitness instructor, I work with people battling physical and other illnesses who seek lifestyle transformation, as well as guiding clients to achieve life-changing relationship, career, and other goals. I created and facilitate the full-day workshop SuperHero Revolution; I co-created and co-facilitate Superwoman Survival Seminar, a women's self-defense and empowerment workshop. In 2016, I graduated from Accomplishment Coaching, an ICF (International Coach Federation) accredited program.

Website: www.michaelroberteck.com

"They seized a challenging situation and transformed it into a time for the whole family to be present and grow together, more connected than ever before."

MICHAEL ROBERT ECK

San Diego, California, United States

CHAPTER 4

The Courage to Evolve

DENISE M. SIMPSON, M.ED.

Life is change...whether we like it or not, and whether we embrace it with courage or have it forced upon us. From the moment we are born our bodies, minds, hearts, and emotions are evolving. In 2020, across the globe humans are being challenged to evolve as we struggle with a global pandemic of COVID-19.

In late February 2020, I was recovering from a cold. As a Chamber of Commerce Ambassador I enjoyed a networking meeting on March 12th shaking hands, then sitting across from a woman who was coughing and hacking. I coughed too. We joked that, "It's a cold, but I don't have COVID-19."

The next day I felt well enough to babysit my 8-year old nephew Caleb in Massachusetts. The long-standing joke in the family is how often I'd babysit, then catch whatever virus he brought home from school-only this time he wasn't sick.

The same day, Friday, March 13th, President Trump declared a National Emergency about the "Novel Coronavirus Disease Outbreak." On Saturday, babysitting duties over, I drove home to New Hampshire, but felt off. With every mile that passed, I was getting sicker and sicker. Something was definitely wrong.

Wham! Sunday morning I was struggling to breathe. Whatever this respiratory illness was it came on hard. I began canceling all my coaching appointments for the upcoming week. Was it just bronchitis, pneumonia, or could it be COVID-19? I didn't know.

Since 2012, I haven't watched network or cable television, so the only news I heard was from friend's phone calls, or what I read from blurbs on the internet. COVID-19 news was evolving daily: its root cause, emergence, transmission, projected spread, physical impact, treatments, and death statistics. Then came the economic, travel, and life-changing impacts as well. The data was evolving.

On Monday, May 16th my regular albuterol inhaler wasn't providing relief and I knew I had a temperature. I called my doctor's office for an appointment and reassurance, but the Physician's Assistance commanded, "Do not come to the office! We will not test you! Do not go to the ER. We need it for emergency personnel." The Physician's Assistant and subsequent doctors who called me on the phone sounded panicked, sometimes contradicting treatment advice over the next three weeks as policies shifted. The medical system I counted on was in disarray. I felt adrift and was still struggling to breathe. The COVID-19 pandemic was evolving with massive confusion.

During a 7-week span, I placed four telehealth calls, was prescribed six medications, and three times was denied COVID-19 testing. During my self-quarantine, I fought for breath and had lots of time to think about how life challenges us. We must evolve how we live our daily lives, what our priorities are, and what really matters.

As a person sensitive to drugs, I was loopy a good portion of the day with way too much binge-watching on Netflix, naps, and in my less coherent states wondered whether this was a planet-wide social experiment. Were governments trying to determine just how much control they had over the populace? I rationalized in my drug-induced fog that it could be good practice in case humanity needed to band together against an alien invasion. This hypothesis didn't go over well when talking to a friend, so I kept it to myself thereafter.

Coughing was the worst part and not having any energy. I lay in bed the first four weeks struggling to breathe and not cough because it hurt-everywhere. It felt like I was trying to cough from the bottom of my lungs upward. I lay there and pondered the value of life, the best ways to treat my body, and what legacy I would leave behind if I did die. I did nothing but sleep, get up to feed my three cats, use the bathroom, and force myself to ingest fluids and eat some food. It was as if the oxygen molecules had been filtered from the air I was breathing like caffeine filtered from coffee. Coughs wracked my body while my back and sides ached proving I had more muscles than I knew.

My life energy dropped to zero, it felt like. Would I always feel like an old woman barely making it downstairs to wash a load of laundry? That was not what I had in mind for the next twenty or thirty years. Health is a state of feeling vitally alive. People routinely comment on my high energy. This shell wasn't me.

My business was closed for weeks now. I spent days in a brain fog preventing any meaningful work on the computer. My car sat unused so that by March 19th Robyn texted me, "Just wanted to check in and see how you are?"

"Who's Robyn?," I wondered. Then I realized it was my next door neighbor who had looked after my cats for me a year ago. She was concerned after seeing no movement for days.

"No, I'm sick," I replied, the understatement of the new millennium.

"Don't hesitate to ask if you need anything at all. We're always at home these days," she offered. Clearly a sign of the times. Robyn and Kris, along with my friend Maureen and her daughter, became my life line to receive groceries and medications.

Surrender to a Shift in Perception

Getting sick became a life-changing process for me. I surrendered to focus only on my health.

I learned valuable lessons when people started calling after I disappeared from my regular Chamber of Commerce meetings, the CoWerc building where I rent an office, and Facebook. It was amazing to me that so many offers of assistance came in. People cared about me. I mattered. I received the gift of realizing I am loved. My perception evolved.

Humility, Help, and Mother Nature

Another lesson was that I needed to humble myself to accept help. I just couldn't do much of anything for myself. I was too ill. No shopping, cleaning, or washing clothes. No networking or coaching calls. Talking more than five minutes caused coughing spasms and short circuited calls from my friend and sister, so it became really quiet at home-really, really quiet. Lots of time to listen to the chatter in my mind.

Courage in the Darkest Hour

Surrender came on a night in the darkest hours when I struggled to breathe, feeling alone and scared. Courage came with the morning light as I decided to focus on healing-and used my arsenal of holistic treatments along with the prescription and over the counter drugs.

Nature's Medicine Cabinet

After learning that hospitals use Vitamin C in IV treatments for respiratory infections, I ramped up my intake of a fizzy Vitamin C supplement drink from 1,000 mg a day to 4,000, 5,000, 7,000 and then 12,000-mg over five days. Whatever the body can't absorb, it eliminates it so I wasn't worried about overdosing. And I felt a marked improvement afterwards, but it wasn't the only treatment.

To boost my Vitamin D production for respiratory functioning I sat outside in the sun for 15-30 minutes. In New Hampshire in early Spring there is still a chill in the air so I needed a blanket, but I was committed to getting better so I forced myself to get out of bed and lift my face to the sun. In my heart I gave thanks to God / The Universe that I wasn't in the hospital on a respirator.

In addition to two prescription cough suppressants, I ingested Elderberry syrup and Chaga mushroom extract, made protein smoothies, and increased my fluid intake. Additionally, I used Albuterol then steroid inhalers. I used a professional nebulizer to fill the bedroom with pure tea tree, peppermint and lemon essential oils. Tea Tree is reported to have antibacterial, antiviral, anti-inflammatory and analgesic properties. The peppermint oil helped to open my airways and the lemon oil lifted my mood. These were undiluted, high-grade oils and they worked! I was breathing easier, and boy, did that raise my hopes.

Self-care Becomes a Sacred Priority

My priorities evolved to focus on sacred self-care: No stress, increase my water intake, ingest food as medicine, sleep whenever my body got drowsy (and that was a lot!), and use Tapping, meditation, and hypnosis recordings to alter my brain waves from stressed out Beta into Theta/Alpha, which accessed my subconscious mind for relaxation and healing. Instead of network television with news stories flashing red statistics to scare me, I listened to meditation music on YouTube. I even refused to hear all the fear-mongering being promulgated from loved ones who called.

I knew from past experience that watching the same traumatic events contributes to anxiety, depression, and PTSD. So seeing the same murders, deaths, and natural disasters on network television wasn't my choice. My friend's anxiety levels were also increasing over the weeks as daily she was glued to national news.

I knew I didn't want to hear about news that was too sensationalized, and inundate my energy field with it. My goal was to build my immune system up, not degrade it. As my friends' anxiety increased, the duration of phone calls with her decreased. It was self-preservation for recovery that mattered more. And I was self-quarantined so I didn't need to know more.

Does this sound selfish? I was too sick to even give that judgment any weight; I felt no guilt either. My priorities had evolved as had my approaches to recovery. I only cared about breathing and recovering my strength. My muscle tone was flaccid after four weeks of bedrest.

Mindset as a Key to Healing

My mindset evolved from being a victim to declaring "I will get better." During phone calls to check on my status by my friend Liz, my sister, and others I stated that my focus was looking forward. I cut short discussions of my symptoms to redirect: "Let's talk about the positives," I told them.

Focus On Rebuilding Strength

"I will get stronger," was the next milestone mantra to focus upon as I forced myself to start bringing mountains of dirty linens to the basement to wash. One trip sapped my strength, a nap was required after the effort, and I allowed it.

Gratitude - A Daily Practice

"I am grateful for…" became a ritual throughout the day relishing how my body moved, the pleasure of hearing birds sing, gazing at the beauty of flowers sprouting through the soil, and appreciating the rising energy of life itself with Springtime erupting. I noticed more of the world around me than the limited real estate of my bed as in the early weeks. My awareness was evolving.

"Thank you" became easier to say after receiving groceries on the porch every few days from Robyn and Kris. As stories emerged globally of people helping people, I gained hope.

Humanity Evolving Into Compassion

Hearing about Italian opera singers filling the spring air from their balconies to entertain their neighbors, spontaneous food banks cropping up in neighborhoods, or postings on Facebook for extra supplies free of charge it became clear to me that humanity was evolving into compassion. People were connecting in ways unthought of or deemed impossible just two months before. My mood lifted higher and my heart lightened as I heard about these stories.

"Self-quarantine, unprecedented times, PPE, social distancing" are all terms we became familiar with. Our way of life was changing. How we respond to evolve with the times is both an individual and a collective process. It can be a blessing or a curse depending on the individual and humanity as a whole. Never before have humans focused on a cause in a collective mindset, but it can be a beautiful process.

Humans can evolve, goodness can overcome mistrust, fear, and hatred. Love is the highest quality inside us.

Challenges test our mindset, character, priorities, mission in life and whether we're connected to our soul's purpose or not. Challenges can be the key to unlocking our Divine Connection in a transformative way or send us into despair that is hell on earth.

The Blessing of Reflection

Now, I feel blessed to have undergone a process of transformation where I paused and reflected on who I am, what I stand for, what I want my legacy to be...and how I can best serve humanity on my journey in this lifetime. Oh sure, it wasn't exactly chosen by me...but it is serving its purpose. This process of reflection is a soul's evolution which impacts the mind, heart, body, and emotions. Lifelong patterns can shift and change in a short time frame when the trigger is a big one, or the resistance is small.

My hope is that others have taken the opportunity to do the same in 2020. My coaching clients made great use of the tools and processes they learned before the Pandemic hit. They had practiced reducing stress, calming the mind, sensing their bodies sensations to direct actions. Because we had explored their life patterns and "Kinky Thinking"-cognitive distortions and improved them-they were able to remain centered, grounded, and function more effectively while other family and friends fell apart.

The entrepreneurs and busy professional moms cocooned with their family, partners and children. They dusted off cookbooks, crockpots, and cookware to spend time creating family dinners. Teaching their children to cook became an enhanced way to connect hearts, minds, and make memories. Life slowed down suddenly the role of chauffeur disappeared. Juggling different school, sport, and work schedules became simplified. Board games came off the shelf and more communication is in play in their households now.

Sure, they were also tensions, anxieties, and worries that cropped up. For couples there was more strain. Some were able to build a greater intimacy as they prioritized protecting their family from harm, while discovering new levels of authenticity in each other. Their relationships evolved.

Evolve with Courage

Evolving new ways of being, of relating, of thinking and feeling are crucial. 2020 is a year of evolution and it can be as easy and natural using one's courage, or as difficult as one makes it with fear. Change is inevitable. One needs interpersonal skills to manage it with ease. New knowledge can be attained and skills can be learned. New ways of navigating life can be implemented for greater success versus struggle. I learned that and have taken it to heart.

My dream is that we, as humans, come together with more compassion, generosity of spirit, forgiveness and release of past hurts and trauma to love in the present moment. This is what I stand for and being The Courageous Heart Coach is who I am, but that is not all of who I am. I am also a daughter, sister, aunt, friend, teacher, artist, gardener, photographer, and lover of cats. I am funny, quirky, smart, creative, adventurous, driven, and a life-long learner. I am intuitive and divine. I AM a being first and a "doing" in between. That's way different than the workaholic I once was in a soul-sucking corporate job where I was harassed...no divinity there except to get me out and on my healing journey. It took courage, but I left, wrote a book, and started two businesses.

Courage is needed to face our personas, the busy distractions we use to cover up the shadow voices that keep us limited from shining our greatest radiance. Connecting the soul to the mind and heart while healing the body is the greatest success in life that any one can achieve-and from this all successes can arise.

Coaching clients is my purpose, my blessing and fills my heart. Awesome Life Coaching is open for business again, and I'm fulfilling my soul purpose. Today I'm clearer than ever what my God-given gifts are, and know it's a travesty not to fully embody and utilize them. Seeing clients embrace a new mindset, become empowered, confident, and communicate with more authenticity is a thrill to me as they step into their True Selves-the best version of who they can be in all their glory. And they love it too. They are humans who are evolving and amplifying their DNA.

As people we sometimes forget we are a biological organism just as a worm, a whale, or an ape is. Over eons life emerged from a primordial soup of single-celled organisms to evolve into the creatures that roam the earth today-including humans. We are not exempt from evolution and it takes courage to navigate more easily. Did I have COVID-19? I don't know, but I do know there are blessings to be gained in 2020 by evolving with courage. I wonder what will yours be?

ABOUT DENISE

Denise M. Simpson, M.Ed., CCH helps coaches, entrepreneurs, and professionals transform their mindset, health, and creative blocks, reducing stress, using courage for bold actions, building confidence, and creating success with more fun. Clients say "that was amazing...a miracle...magical" as they get peak results from the Courageous Heart Living™ Program within Awesome Life Coaching.

Denise coaches globally with two Masters of Education, is a Certified Evolutionary Mystic Meditation™ Facilitator, Certified Soul Entrainment Facilitator and EFT Practitioner, Tapping Into Wealth™ coach, NGH Consulting Hypnotist and Convention faculty, speaker, and author of A Muse Your Self Writing™ on Amazon. Denise applies her years of education, expertise, and global award-winning training skills to deliver awesome results so you can live an awesome life!

Website: www.denisemsimpson.com/chl-gift-set

"Connecting the soul to the mind and heart while healing the body is the greatest success in life that any one can achieve-and from this all successes can arise."

DENISE M. SIMPSON, M.ED.

New Hampshire, United States

CHAPTER 5

Rediscovering My Voice

ANNE COLLIN

Singing has been my main form of self expression for as long as I can remember. I found solace in using my voice to perform, to receive approval, and to navigate through the intensity of my emotions. My grandmother taught me my first song, "Oh, You Beautiful Doll," when I was two years old. I know this because my aunt still has a cassette tape dated 1980 on which my two-year-old voice can be heard singing it in its entirety:

"Oh, you beautiful doll!

You great, big, beautiful doll!

Let me put my arms about you,

I could never live without you.

Oh, you beautiful doll!

You great, big, beautiful doll!

If you ever leave me how my heart will ache,

I want to hug you but I'm scared you'll break.

Oh, oh, oh, oh,

Oh, you beautiful doll!"

(Lyrics by Seymour Brown; public domain)

At the end of the recording, I can be heard demanding, "I want to hear the baby sing," referring to myself—I wanted my grandmother to rewind the tape and let me hear my own voice.

When COVID-19 first hit the news, I wasn't afraid at all. Perhaps naively after fifteen years as a public elementary school music teacher, I assumed that I had built up strong enough immunities to withstand whatever new germs might come my way. I would carry on and wash my hands more frequently.

But when, for the first time in all of those years, my school closed its doors in the middle of a normal week in March, I panicked. How long would this last? Would I ever see my students again? Was the National Guard coming to my town to make sure I didn't leave my house? Would I be able to see my family or my friends? Even writing about how I felt that day over two months ago, I feel the familiar shortness of breath, tightness in my chest, and tingling sensations in my arms that come with extreme anxiety for me.

The most difficult aspect of facing down that uncertainty was that I was suddenly bereft of the one outlet from which I had always derived comfort, and with which I strive to bring comfort to others. When would I get to sing with my choir again? When would I be able to perform in a musical with my friends? My voice has always been a source of accomplishment and pride, as well as a safe way for me to communicate my emotions. I would joke, "music is the love that never leaves." Without that outlet, it was even more challenging to process my fears about the pandemic. I felt as if I had been completely stripped of all of my positive coping mechanisms. The love that was never supposed to leave had taken a time out, after all. I felt like Ariel, having just signed over her voice to Ursula the sea witch.

During those first days that soon became weeks and then months, I struggled to find new ways to cope. I worked with my colleagues to transform our curriculum into online distance learning. I began having Google meetings with my students and singing popular songs with them. I recorded covers of songs from the privacy of my home. I participated in live streaming performances and "virtual" choirs, in which I sang alone and then added my video submissions to bigger projects. I was grateful for those opportunities, but I missed the exchange of energy that occurs when you are blending your voice with other voices: when a conductor gestures to you to make a vocal entrance; when you feel that you have moved an audience or uplifted them. I longed for the day I would feel that connection again.

The first time I was given the opportunity to sing outside of my house came on May 31, 2020–Pentecost Sunday. I don't consider myself a particularly religious person, preferring more to stay home and practice spirituality in my own way. However, I was raised in the Catholic Church and started singing in the choir with my aunt as choir director and organist when I was 4 years old. I have sung for Catholic, Episcopalian, Congregational, and Unitarian Universalist services countless times.

Pentecost is the celebration of when Jesus' disciples received the Holy Spirit, which led them to begin preaching. It's regarded as the birth of the church—in other words, when the disciples found their voices.

I was invited to sing an Episcopal service that morning. The invitation came from the director of a choir I sing with—a choir that had to cancel the remainder of its season due to the pandemic. I was excited to see my friend and to perform at his church, where I had sung several times before. When I received that email, I replied an immediate "yes." I didn't know what singing in church would be like with church still being closed to the public, but I was more than ready to give it a try.

When I arrived at the church that morning, my friend greeted me. It turned out that only four of us were there—the priest, the organist (my friend, who would also give the readings), someone helping to set up the camera, and me. After a brief rehearsal and some technical troubleshooting, the service went as it normally does, minus the congregants who would normally have gathered in person rather than from the privacy of their own homes via Facebook Live.

Despite their absence, I tried to imagine the people who tuned in to listen to the mass and thought of myself sending them a few minutes of peace through the hymns I sang to an almost empty church, standing before a ring light and an iPhone on a tripod.

When it came time for the sermon, the priest spoke about current events as they related to Pentecost. The Holy Spirit is sometimes referred to as the breath of God, or breath of life. Less than a week before, on May 25, 2020, George Floyd, a black man accused of using a counterfeit 20-dollar bill, was suffocated by a white police officer who knelt on his neck for 8 minutes and 46 seconds despite Floyd's pleas that he couldn't breathe. Three other officers stood by and declined to come to his aid.

As I listened to the sermon, I was moved to tears thinking about how George Floyd and people of color feel voiceless all the time—not just during a pandemic, like I did because I wasn't able to do the creative work I normally do in the same way that I usually do it—but in their daily routines, as they navigate their way through a world that looks at them with unfounded suspicion and, in many tragic cases such as that of George Floyd, does not honor and recognize the dignity and light in them as fellow humans.

I may not be a religious person, but the concept of the Holy Spirit resonates with me—that invisible surge of energy that connects us all and inspires us to call on our creative strengths to communicate with one another and to offer support and kindness. I had been trying to suppress the fear of not knowing when I would be able to see my students and my friends and family again due to the pandemic, but I don't know the same fear as a black man being pulled over by the police, or the worry that parents of black children must feel.

As a musician, the ways that I can be of service are more emotional in nature than tangible outcomes. I sing to children. I sing to people in places of worship. I sing to theater-goers looking to escape the real world for a while. However, music itself is a universal language that transcends barriers. As I lent my voice to the mass that morning, I reflected on other ways that I could be of service through listening and through spreading messages of inclusivity. The closing hymn that day was an African-American spiritual dating back to before the civil war:

"Every time I feel the spirit moving in my heart, I will pray."

Music is my prayer. Music is the love that never leaves. Music is the voice of the voiceless. Music is the breath of God—or, if God is an uncomfortable concept for some, music is the inalienable and immortal breath of life.

As we begin to see the pandemic winding down, my hope is that we will all take this opportunity to reflect on the ways that we can use our voices to bring each other comfort and to speak up against injustice.

The moments that I found the most comforting since COVID-19 swept the world and changed my day to day life were the unexpected ones: going on a solitary hike and hearing someone practicing guitar in the distance; seeing cheerful messages scrawled in chalk on driveways; painted rocks left along the street to greet me as I walked; sweet emails and videos of my students singing at home or playing instruments. These small acts of beauty and kindness weren't so small when weighed by the measure of the comfort they brought me in a dark time. We all have the ability within us to spread that light. We can choose to use it through simple acts of service or self-expression, and we can use it to lend strength to the disenfranchised.

It can be all too easy to ignore the power that we have to make a difference when we are busy with the minutiae of our day to day lives. Maybe within the darkness of this pandemic there is a bigger opportunity to reflect inside of ourselves and take the time to slow down and listen to our breath; to hear the quiet voice of the spirit inside us that guides our actions through love.

When I sang in public again for the first time since COVID-19 made us all shutter our doors, I sang in front of only three other people in person and had to imagine the others listening from home, and I missed the collective energy of the parishioners who normally would have been present and listening to me. There are small moments that occur under normal circumstances: a contented sigh or a nod of approval, or perhaps a familiar smiling face of a friend or relative. I had a sense of purpose, but no immediate reception. The church was empty, and it felt a bit eerie.

I can only imagine that being a person of color might feel like singing to an angry audience, with members who outright ignore you or attack you.

My dearest wish is that we will be able to hold one another without fear, just as I sang at two years old. I wish that no one ever had to die crying out for breath or for their mother. I recognize how lucky I am that I don't have to fear for my own life or my son's life due to the color of our skin. The inconvenience of the pandemic aside, I don't know what it's like to have to worry about what will happen if I go near the wrong person. I may have to sing privately for a time to safeguard against the spread of a virus, but in a larger sense, my voice is not perpetually silenced.

As public establishments begin to open their doors again, I hope that privileged people can also begin to open their minds and hearts. I hope that we will use our voices to promote equality, peace, and fair treatment for all, but especially for people of color who have suffered oppression for so long and at times up until their final breaths.

The spirit of life that connects us is the calm voice that inspires us and speaks to us in the stillness to let us know that we are capable of great compassion. Rather than reacting with impatience, we can take this time to reclaim our voices, acknowledging when to sing out, and when to listen.

ABOUT ANNE

Anne Collin is an elementary school music teacher and vocalist based in New Canaan, Connecticut. Anne has her Master of Music in Music Education from Boston University and her Bachelors of Arts in Music from Manhattanville College. When not in the classroom, she may be found on the stage, in a yoga studio, or in a swimming pool.

"Music is the love that never leaves.

Music is the voice of the voiceless."

ANNE COLLIN, M. MUS.

Connecticut, United States

Pivot

leadership

gift

reinvention

creation

blessings

dream

CHAPTER 6

Leadership:
Empathy & Perspective

IAN CHARLERY

As a young entrepreneur seeking to create an organizational culture fostered on accountability, trust, and love, I have actively sought out the message that COVID-19 would teach me. The tragedy that is COVID-19 is teaching us so many lessons. I suspect that even after this global pandemic is over we will still benefit from the lessons that this era has to teach us.

So far what is clear to me is that this pandemic reinforces a major leadership philosophy of mine: Empathy and Perspective. I believe empathy and perspective are cornerstone attributes of great leaders.

Living on an island during this global pandemic can either be an experience in paradise or a nightmare. If you have family here on Grand Cayman, then you know for certain you will be okay because worst case, you can get food from them and if you get sick at least you know that someone on island has your back. However, if you do not benefit from this fortune, your situation is grim.

When an island goes into a 24-hour lockdown with curfews ranging from HARD (leaving your home is prohibited during those hours) and SOFT (you are only allowed to leave home on your letter day). Persons with the last name between A-K can leave home on Mondays, Wednesdays, and Fridays the other days for the remaining letters. Supermarkets and banks will only accept you if it is your letter day. The transportation system is completely shut down. So if you depended on taking a bus to get to the grocery store you would need to find alternative means which usually translates to walking because...well...social distancing. So, essentially, you are a prisoner in your residence unable to leave at your own will. On top of this, your landlord is writing you letters reminding you of his first letter sent at the beginning of the pandemic; advising that if you are unable to work that you should leave her place or the island because she has her mortgage obligations that trump your lack of work problem.

During the pandemic thousands of expatriate workers had to seek aid from the government due to being relieved from their jobs. Thousands were homeless and unable to leave to return to their own countries because our borders and their country's borders were closed. They were trapped here with no money, no shelter, no food, and the increased risk for infection. These combined factors gave rise to a serious humanitarian crisis in the Cayman Islands. Charities were reignited and the effort was on the way to provide much-needed aid to those in need; however, charities struggled to meet the increasing demand as the number of unemployed due to COVID-19 grew dramatically.

The impact of the pandemic cannot be overstated. All business stops when an island goes into 24-hour lockdown. For a young company like ours these moments could be make or break for us. We apply a Blue Ocean strategy in our business which simply means we do not form our business strategy off of what our "competitors" are doing. Our leadership focus is Authentic and Sustainable leadership and for this reason our actions may not align with the more popular decisions of releasing staff and thereby our responsibility to them.

Who I am as a leader is something I take very seriously. I am always striving to be the best father, husband, son, and leader. I believe in walking in a person's shoes and really doing my best to understand from their perspective.

Walking in Another's Shoes

I speak a lot about trying to walk in someone's shoes to understand them but one person whose shoes I know I could never walk in, partly because they are heels but mostly because they are too big to fill. I know I could not walk a mile in my mother's shoes; the mere thought sends a jolt through my body. I have seen firsthand some of the magic that she has created and I have heard legendary stories about her brilliance.

As a girl she barely had shoes and would have to travel over 20 miles to school by foot. With no transportation and such a long distance she would often walk or run to school. Sometimes she would get a ride via motor car, this was rare but it was a relief at times. Some days, she would miss school to focus on helping her grandfather on the farm which was the main source of income. Planting vegetables, caring for the animals, whatever was needed and was asked of her, she completed. Both of her parents lived apart from each other. They both worked and ensured she was provided for. Her mother resided permanently in Barbados whilst her father resides in St. Lucia in a different household than her. On the days that she did go to school she would be ostracized and scorned for not having the textbooks. Being from a poor background, my mother left school without much school education but make no mistake, school is only one form of education. My mother's brilliance and bravery were key characteristics that assisted her in being the world's best mom.

During the pandemic there has been an increased feeling of family and togetherness. Even with complete strangers I have noticed a connection and the emphasis that we have to make sacrifices for each other. For instance, we wear masks to protect others not for ourselves but because there is a chance that we could be saving a life. These are my thoughts during the pandemic. Let us take some more imaginary steps in my mother's shoes.

Her bravery and brilliance really spoke when she decided to migrate to the Cayman Islands in search of something better. She had acquired bartending skills when she worked at the hotel and realized that this profession brought with it the opportunity to make extra money through tips. Those tips would later fund her travel and literally my entire life.

I cannot remember a time when my mother put herself first or wanted something for herself. She would make it obvious and clear that every move she made was to ensure that I would have the chances that she did not have. That was her entire mission. She worked long grueling double, triple and sometimes even quadruple shifts coming home exhausted only to sleep for a few hours to return to work and do it again. For me. Her only child.

In moments of crisis, the cream rises to the top. The pandemic has me thinking about the last time there was an island-wide curfew. The last major crisis, Hurricane Ivan, was a category 5 hurricane that ripped and destroyed the Cayman Islands on September 11, 2004. Over 80% of the island was destroyed. CNN reported that the island had disappeared off the radar screen. For a moment, it was thought that the Cayman Islands was lost, swallowed into the ocean.

The powerful hurricane winds ripped our apartment to shreds sending our roof into another neighborhood. The water was everywhere! This crisis was like no other. My mother, though, was calm, brave, and gave me the feeling that everything would be okay despite the destruction around us. We lost every single thing we owned. Years of savings went down the drain, but we rebuilt our lives. To this day the memory of her leadership stands tall in my mind. She would say, "Things are things but people matter more. We are healthy and not injured. It could be a lot worse."

She was right, it could be worse. With no work and no sign of work restarting the situation looked more and more grim. We were homeless and jobless, in what still felt like a foreign country at the time. The truth is, I was never worried not once. We picked up the pieces bit by bit and slowly rebuilt our lives. Growing up we were never really attached to material things. Once we had each other we knew that we would be okay. I remember her saying she could not imagine going through this hurricane without knowing that I was safe. It was as if that would have been more painful than anything she could have experienced during the most powerful hurricane in the Island's history.

Sometimes as children we fail to see the sacrifices our parents have made for our betterment and safety. This global pandemic has brought me closer to those sacrifices. My once crazily busy schedule dropped down to a snail's pace. The Great Pause provided countless opportunities to reconnect with myself and some of those sacrifices that were made so that I could be here in that very moment. I always appear to come out of those meditations energized and clear-headed.

The sacrifices our parents have made for us is exactly why we have achieved the things that we have already achieved and will achieve in the future.

The ultimate display of love is to sacrifice. To leave your comfort in search of discomfort so that your seed may reap the harvest of your sacrifice. My mother's parents left her in search of better economic impact. My mother left me in search of the same mission as her parents but despite being told it would be hard or impossible to take me along she made it happen; although the challenges cannot be overstated. She really gave up a lot to ensure that I was safe and that I had a chance.

You see, while you have heard about my mother's journey very briefly, you could replicate this story for 100 percent of my staff. The majority of them share the exact same or similar story to that of my mother. Ninety-five percent migrated from another country in search of better support for their family. Some of them come from as far as Nepal, Nicaragua, Jamaica, Guyana, Honduras, India, and Nigeria. Each of them supports up to five people in their home country. Some of them have had to take loans amongst their families in order to fund their way to the Cayman Islands where they will work in the cleaning industry and other similar industries. Each payday they would leave themselves with just enough money to cover their basic needs and would send the remaining funds to their country to take care of their families and pay back the loans that funded their migration. The majority would be sending funds to ensure their children were in school and could afford the textbooks, food, and other supplies that their children would need to be successful at school- much like how my mother did for me when I went to school in Jamaica.

My move to Jamaica was necessary since an application to remain on island and attend school would be turned down by the Immigration Department. My mother did not give up and so I was off to Jamaica for school which meant my mother had to work extra hard because now I would have to attend a boarding school which came at a price clearly out of a regular bartender's scope. There was nothing regular about my mother and so she made it work and when the family that I lived with asked for more money she agreed and when the school asked her for a high tuition she agreed. All because she was dedicated to ensuring that I had the opportunities she did not have. My mother and my staff share the same actions, sacrificing herself for me.

I often wish I appreciated her sacrifice more. She pushed herself so that I would not be left behind.

They work hard, they save their money, and they forgo their happiness all as an act of love to their families back home. Sometimes they are homesick and sad for months and years even. You inquire genuinely as you see their somber moods. They hesitate to share and you cannot blame them. Opening up is not easy for everyone but as a leader you learn to create a safe space for vulnerability, so that when your team is down and in need of encouragement and support, they can receive it and also give it because even leaders need encouragement.

The laws restrict low-income workers like cleaners, bartenders etc. from having their children on island as their ability to care for another person is brought into question based on their pay. As a result they are often in a strange land on their own much like my mother would have been if my stepfather was not present. Unfortunately, many of my team do not have the support of a spouse on the island. Who is their emergency contact?

Imagine being unable to list an emergency contact? We stand as the emergency contact for all of our staff. In the past, we have had to make contact with families of our staff who are overseas. It did not take COVID-19 to remind us that cleaners are essential workers. Without them we would be in a big mess, pun intended. Clearly we have become so disconnected from our humanity that we do not notice the janitors, we do not even say hello or good morning until we need something. This sort of behavior has to stop. We will not always get it right but we have to make an effort to be better each day and sometimes it means we just have to be in the NOW. Being present is what grants us the ability to connect with anyone.

Let us say you are working late enough to meet the cleaners and that night you are walking out of your elevator and passing the cleaner. Be present enough to say hello. You do not need to stop and have a full conversation but the decent thing to do is acknowledge another human being. The cleaners do not need or want your pity! They just want to be treated like human beings and not tools or machines with no souls to clean up your mess. Some of you who might be reading this may find it hard to believe the experience some of my team has had with clients. Some would throw the trash on the ground in front of them and ask them to pick it up. Others would deliberately berate the staff. I recall this one instance where the customer was upset that the cleaner had the same brand cellular phone as him. He questioned her until his stance was clear. How dare you and I share any part of the same world!? Needless to say those customers who mistreat our staff are no longer customers because we know who our most important customers are: our staff!

Could you imagine your mother apprehensive to go to work because her client constantly talks down to her and treats her less than? Yeah, me NEITHER! If it is not good enough for my mother then it is not good enough for anyone on my team. As far as customer service is concerned, you are the disrespect you fail to correct. So we have a strict policy with our staff. The customer is under no circumstances to disrespect you. Money is not more valuable than your humanity.

A company must stand in solidarity with its employees. Employees are trained and are made aware of the company's policies and guidelines. A company's actions will form its identity, so during the global pandemic, A1 Cleaning Services, catered to its most important customers.

Our Most Important Customers

If your customer was in desperate need of your service would you turn your back on them? Moreover, if you turned your back on them what message would that be sending to the customers that are still under your portfolio? Would you expect these remaining customers to ignore your actions and ultimately your reputation?

It is true, economic freedom is the driving factor behind capitalism. People need money and will work under the harshest conditions in order to attain money to attend to their needs. This however does not make it acceptable to place them under harsh working conditions.

Think back to a time you worked in a job that you did not feel appreciated or valued. What would happen if you felt valued and were provided with more opportunities for economic freedom which ultimately during a global Pandemic translates to having your most basic needs of safety, food, health, and connection met.

What If instead of turning your back on your customer you extended a helping hand? Would that be considered authentic and sustainable leadership?

During the global pandemic that is COVID-19, A1 Cleaning Services dedicated itself to caring for our most important customers, our staff. Seeing the smiles on their faces and the feeling of community amongst our company immediately proves that we made the right decision by providing critical coverage to all staff.

During the pandemic, our organization committed the following to its VIP customers, our staff:

- All rents paid. (No mental burden of worrying if you will be homeless.)
- All health insurance kept active. (To be sick in a foreign land with no medical insurance is tough for anyone.)
- Monthly food packages delivered to each staff to reduce

their need to travel during the pandemic.

Cornerstones of Great Leadership: Empathy & Perspective

During a global pandemic no one really knows what leadership will be needed. Some may have a guess, but until recently few really knew what was required to lead an organization through a global pandemic. However, does that mean they get a pass if their leadership is not up to par? I wonder what impact this would have on an organization.

Business owners must apply sustainable decision-making especially during the time of a global pandemic. Sustainable decisions are decisions that have a lasting positive impact. Entrepreneurs of today must apply this sort of thought process if they wish to create a culture that creates an environment that people want to be a part of. Only with empathy and perspective can they imagine themselves in their employees' shoes and only by achieving this connection will they be able to gain or strengthen their relationships with their employees. The benefits of a strong organizational culture are astronomical. When people feel trusted and appreciated they work harder and are more receptive to feedback. Simply put, your leadership actions can contribute to a growth mindset within your employees. The actions of the leadership resonates throughout every crevice of an organization. If your leader screams and ridicules his team then the junior leaders or managers will do the same. What you do and say matters and it determines how far your leadership will progress your team and ultimately the entire organization.

My hope is that more organizations move toward authentic and sustainable leadership because those are the practices that will transform our business culture into one that works alongside each other and not seemingly on top of each other.

The Cayman Islands on the 24th of July, 2020 reported ZERO

active cases of the Coronavirus for the first time since the beginning of March 2020. When it mattered most we were there for each other and that is something we can all be proud of.

About Ian

Ian Charlery is a father, friend, husband, and son. He is also the CEO of A1 Cleaning Services and helps lead a team of professionals who successfully deliver commercial and residential cleaning services. Ian embodies authentic and servant leadership and is a champion for businesses focused on serving their most important customers, their staff and the environment. Ian is a certified life coach and holds a Masters Degree in Business Management. He believes that finding the balance between doing and being is the essence of the human experience.

"My hope is that more organizations move toward authentic and sustainable leadership because those are the practices that will transform our business culture."

Ian Charlery

Grand Cayman, Cayman Islands

CHAPTER 7

A Course Corrected

CHRISTINE A. MOLA

My true awakening began Friday, March 20, 2020 at 10:30am when the COVID-19 came to town, abruptly forcing the hand of layoffs to 95 associates at the hotel where I was a Director in the sales department, to include me. There were no furloughs for us. We were terminated without notice. Tears, fear, and anxiety crept in throughout my department, not just for those that were part of Phase 1 terminations, but for those left behind knowing what their fate was. I gathered my office wares fitting in two boxes and was gracefully walked out by coworkers in tears leaving me with hugs and kisses; there was no social distancing in place yet, we could still FEEL what was happening to us individually, and collectively. This was the first day of the rest of my life, and ironically, my Gift.

I spent fifteen of my twenty-five year professional career, to date, in the hospitality industry within central Connecticut and surrounding regions. It has always been a competitive industry in small square mile areas concentrated with competitive venues. But who knew that one "teeny tiny virus" could take down a billion-dollar industry in two weeks' time, nationally and worldwide? Not me, and certainly no one else as it came upon us like a terrific windstorm with nothing to ground us, and no end in sight. With that, it was no coincidence that I had spent the previous five months fearfully contemplating my departure from the very industry that was "setting me free." Little did I know that this "teeny tiny virus" was about to save my life, and Course Correct my future.

As I am only human, all of this left me pretty pissed off for a couple of days. I had a pity party, or two, then in my typical form, jumped back up and started to forge ahead, but this time it was different. I had time, with nowhere to go! What do I do now? Oh, did I forget to mention that I had just left, two weeks prior to my layoff, a growingly challenged six-and-a-half-year relationship that needed time mending? Yes, because 2020 was MY TIME to begin again! SUPERWOMAN!

I found a lovely two-family house in my hometown, a stone's throw from my family, occupying the first floor, along with my oldest daughter Ashley, who lives with autism. With the fear now permeating of this rapidly spreading COVID-19 virus, and the new stay-at-home quarantine orders unfolding, it was starting to become a whole new world, over night!

Social distancing came into focus as a new normal, (God only knew at that point what was about to unfold), so my children's dad and I decided it best that Ashley quarantine with Grandma for a few weeks and see what happens, as Dad and I were still in the public, exposed to this nightmare. That left just me in my new home, all by my lonesome, settling into what would be a two-and-a-half month 'Corona Q,' which became my colorful reference to the Great Pause.

Well now, where did we go from here? Lives interrupted without notice, "normal" daily tasks and agendas coming to a halt. Life undone. Time to assimilate; there is no try, just do! As so much upheaval in daily existence was unfolding universally, for some, this Great Pause was a blessing creating forced endings to misdirected paths. I for one had taken a big giant step in February of 2020 reclaiming my independence.

However, I was still settling for a job that was completely unfulfilling. Out of fear, I miserably rooted myself, convinced it just may be too late for a new start; which was uncharacteristic of me.

Yet, ironically, it was *fear of the COVID-19* that created my forced exit from this position resulting in glorious time and space for New Beginnings. The flames of hope were reignited. God and the Universe were sending a message: Humans, rise up! Show us what you are capable of as a people and individuals. This is your chance to shine. Don't disappoint...

I used my two-and-a-half-month gift of time, the CoronaQ, delving into ME, and I knew I was never going to be given this gift for ME in quite this way again, so there was no wasting it! I grounded my spirituality and started to heal personal relationships that went awry and developed brand new relationships with people seeking the same spiritual awakening and enlightenment.

As I continue to refer to this "gift of time" it not only allowed the ability to strengthen myself, but to strengthen my relationship with my youngest daughter Nicole, and my grandchildren Adrian and Annie. I was able to witness the strength of my daughter who left her part-time job to become the stay at home mom, teacher, and creator of fun for her children, aka SUPERHERO! It was *not* an easy transition for any of the young parents in the world, but she did it, and they continue to thrive in the safe home she and my son-in-law created for their children.

I am beamingly proud of my son-in-law who remained at work as an essential worker for a large local grocery store chain where he supervises in the warehouse, over eighty hours a week, along with coworkers assuring that a people in crisis will eat, and of course, have toilet paper! Ashley and Grandma continue to quarantine together at the time I write this, and there is comfort in knowing they are cozy and safe. I was content in knowing my own parents self-sufficiently quarantined themselves in my childhood home they built together, safely taking care of each other.

Adversity was created and swiftly defeated by a shield of might and a sword of strength. What does not kill you...well, you know the rest.

This Great Pause created by the teeny tiny virus named COVID-19 affected each individual and community differently around the world. It has caused great tragedy in many families with loved ones perishing or elongated hospital stays for others with no family or friends to comfort. Other families were separated, communicating by distance only through windows, doors, phones, and video. Businesses and industries were disrupted and/or destroyed. Young mothers and fathers rearranged their whole lives to accommodate their children staying home, becoming teachers to their children as well as 24/7 caregivers.

Senior adults adapted to another type of loneliness, which added to the challenge of aging gracefully. As people suddenly halted, they reconfigured what was habit, and are now building an entire new infrastructure. This was survival of the fittest in its greatest form. It was time that regular folk shed their suits, skirts and heels and become Superheroes in Jammies! (The absolute best kind.)

We celebrated the "unsung hero", our frontline workers of every walk, essential workers had a whole new meaning and purpose. LOVE was abundant in communities worldwide, and though it be ever so fleeting, we do know it really happened.

Humanity: we are a complicated breed, but back us into a corner, and with locked arms stretching across the land, we will unite and overcome adversity with Peace and Love. Love always wins. God and Universe were pleased.

At the end of two and a half months, I was gratefully offered a position within my career expertise in a different yet complementary industry, senior living.

I line the walls of MY new home with CoronaQ artwork from my grandkids and await the day my daughter Ashley can come home so I can hug her long and hard, and never take for granted that warm feeling again. I look forward to the holidays and pray we get to spend them all together celebrating gratitude and joy. I am working on my lifelong dream of being an author and helping people with my word by sharing stories of adversity that I continue to defeat with Faith and Hope, and a whole lot of work!

My purpose in life is unfolding and this is my future. This is the gift of a virus, the Great Pause: a Course Corrected.

About Christine

Christine is a native and lifelong resident of her hometown, Bristol, Connecticut. Christine is blessed with two beautiful daughters, Ashley and Nicole. Christine's professional career has majored in Marketing & Sales in the Hospitality and Events industry. Her professional career, after the COVID-19 disruption, blissfully landed in the senior living community industry. Christine has always been a storyteller, whether it be in her written word of short stories, to the life moment events she created with her professional clients; there was always a beginning, a climactic middle, and a fairy tale ending. Her magical children's book series will soon come to life on paper and she is creating "Anchoring the Transformation," a platform for sharing personal stories of transition.

Email: Bloom23productions@gmail.com

Facebook: Bloom23productions /Anchoring the Transformation

"Humanity; we are a complicated breed, but back us into a corner, and with locked arms stretching across the land, we will unite and overcome adversity with Peace and Love. Love always wins."

Christine A. Mola

Connecticut, United States

CHAPTER 8

Coming to Grips with the COVID-19 Crisis

STEPHEN FOWLER

The COVID-19 crisis (as it has been called by mass media) can be considered from two separate approaches. One is the societal approach and the other is the individual approach. I have chosen to focus on the individual approach.

As a second semester senior during my undergraduate studies at Marist College, I took a course called Philosophy of Education with a professor named Italo Benin. He defined a crisis as a breakdown of a project. The example that he gave was a bit harsh to my thinking, that of a mother who loses a child. While I thought he was critical and could have been more sympathetic, his example did serve a purpose in that it was clear that that specific project has clearly come to an end from a secular perspective. And the question that the professor poses is, "What are you going to do now?"

I'm guessing that most people would agree with me that the example is particularly harsh. Clearly there is going to be a stretch of time during which the person affected is going to have to process their new reality. She is not just going to turn around the next day and join a chess club. However, at some point, she will have to decide if she is going to get on with her life, and if so, how?

For most of us (albeit not all), what we are facing now is not so dire. And right there, we should look to take some comfort. However, there may still be a stretch of time during which we experience disorientation. Nowadays, we talk about the time for processing what has occurred.

The project has broken down. Maybe a job has been lost. Certainly, no one is attending ball games, movies, concerts, or lectures. We have not been to restaurants, the hairdresser, or the library. We Americans are not used to this. The last generation to experience anything like this was that which lived through World War II, and most of them have passed on.

So, how does an individual adapt to this new reality? Especially since we are hearing so much about how things are not going to return to what we recall as being normal? We are being told that there is going to be a new normal.

There are different approaches one can take, but I am going to try to reach out to the reader as one individual to another, to provide you with a little perspective. I am going to share a little bit of my own story.

I worked in the insurance business for twenty-seven years, the last twenty-one of them as a group insurance underwriter, essentially for the same company. I made a decent amount of money doing it (all of which is now gone) but it did not make me happy. At the end of that time, I was laid off. I had a year's severance to lean on, so I tried to get back into the insurance business, but the severance probably contributed to a lack of urgency at first, and I already was experiencing nightmares of my previous work life.

I tried switching careers. I decided I wanted to be a teacher. I took and passed all of the certification exams, volunteered, observed, substituted, and took a number of graduate level courses. I took a position as a tutor in an urban school district. I was hired to teach 6th and 7th grade math in an urban school district, but I lasted less than one month before I was told that I had lost control of the students. I could spend however much time blaming other people or circumstances for the fact that up to now, things have not worked out for me along that career path, but while I have not given up on it, I also recognize the necessity to pay the bills.

With that in mind, I have taken jobs at a large retail store, an amusement park, as a canvasser for a solar company, and with two residential care agencies. Then, this past winter, I was able to convince another solar company to hire me as a rep. I graduated from the sales training in early March, and the next week, I was furloughed, along with all my classmates, due to the coronavirus. We have since all been laid off without benefits. As of this writing, I am delivering meals as an independent contractor for a company that has an app set up for that purpose.

At various times throughout all of this, I found myself dealing with other stresses beyond looking for work during all the times that I was out of it. My spouse has had fragile health throughout this time, and I have lost my dearest friend, a four-legged fellow named Archie who was with me for thirteen years. At one time, I sank into depression to the point where I had determined that I ought to end my time on this earth, and I had determined how to go about it. I spent the better part of a week in a hospital, healing from what would have been called a nervous breakdown two or three generations ago.

I share all of this not to ask for sympathy, but to give the reader some context for how they might go about recovering and moving forward from a breakdown of the project. I recently posted on Facebook that everyone should get fired at least five times. Why? Because we need to come to the realization that losing a job is not the end of the world. Your job does not define who you are.

As cruel as it might seem in retrospect to some people, there is a lesson to be learned by messing up the hill constructed by a colony of ants (as an example). This is something I did as a child. If you watch them long enough, you will observe that at first, they all seem disoriented. They are all running around in different directions. However, they eventually become reorganized, and go about reconstructing their ant hill. There are no exceptions to this phenomenon. It happens every single time. I have no wish to get inside the head of an ant, but I was able to see, even as a small child, that they don't spend a lot of time pointing fingers and assessing blame when their project breaks down. They simply start another project.

And so, we are faced now with redefining ourselves. Are we going to sit around moping? Are we going to play the blame game? Or are we going to dig deep down and find that flexibility and nimbleness of mind that is hardcoded into us? Again, I am not saying that there is not going to be a time of disorientation and frustration. What I am saying is that we all have the capacity for resilience, and for reinventing ourselves. Your conscience, provided to you by a divine creator defines who you are, not your job. There is going to be a new reality. You have a role to play in shaping it. Rise up, dust yourself off, and go. Oh, and don't forget to stop and reevaluate regularly. It is when we go and go and go without checking to see if we are veering off the originally intended direction, that we get into trouble.

About Stephen

Stephen Fowler has studied at the University of Hard Knocks including field work as a caregiver, a math tutor for inner city middle schoolers, a canvasser for a solar company, and most recently as an Instacart shopper. He still finds time to care for his furry four-legged friend, and to play online chess. When he can swing it, he likes to take a few turns on the mountain in the winter months. He is the organist at a Congregational Church and will reconvene the choir there once it is again safe. He is author of the book, "What Do You Think? Conversations about Faith and Spirituality in the New Millennium."

"They don't spend a lot of time pointing fingers and assessing blame when their project breaks down. They simply start another project."

Stephen Fowler

Connecticut, United States

Chapter 9

Lessons from My Journey in the Time of COVID

April Goff Brown

Pre-COVID. Life was easy, quiet, flexible. I had been retired from my full-time career for over two years and was focused on building my jewelry design business and writing a children's book. 2020 was my year to build local connections, network, and get my jewelry carried in a couple of Connecticut-based boutiques. I joined a women's network to get myself out and talking to other like-minded women, women who are entrepreneurs and building their own businesses while supporting others. I joined a group coaching program to build momentum and propel myself forward as I built my business.

I spent most of my days in my studio either creating or working online, maintaining my website, accessing social media, creating marketing posts, building my business page and email list. Even that work was fun because it involved learning and creating, two of my favorite things to do.

I also had written a children's book that had been germinating in my head for four years. A publishing company was interested and I explored other options for publishing. The illustrations were the challenge and finding someone that could translate my story into pictures that met my vision – and that I could afford.

My husband and I had also begun to plan our brief vacation jaunts with our first stop for a few days on Block Island during May. We had been taking short excursions each spring to a local island to be able to walk along the water which was a treat after the long winter. Our ferry reservations were made. The inn was booked.

2020 was progressing nicely. Life was good.

Then COVID-19 hit and life as I knew it changed.

EARLY COVID. Social distancing? No problem. My introverted self naturally socially distanced so it wasn't going to be a problem. I made infrequent appointments to go out and was happy to spend most of my days alone in my own world, creating and tending my business. Social media kept me in touch, emails and texts did too.

When schools closed for a couple of weeks in early March, I seized the chance to spend time with my seven year-old granddaughter, Olivia. Her parents still were working and I relished the time to spend with her every day. I'd set up my dining room as her classroom and worked at creating a schedule for us to follow each day. She spent nights here too and it felt like a vacation for her. After lessons, we had an "after-school" program which was mainly playing games, doing projects up in my studio, and baking. My days were L-O-N-G as Olivia wanted all my attention all of the time. Then school was cancelled until the end of March. Then it was cancelled for the remainder of the school year.

The women in my network were being encouraged to pivot our businesses and figure out how to make it work online. Groups began to sprout everywhere. Everyone wanted to help. Early on, I participated in an online shopping event with a few other like-minded entrepreneurs which was fun and successful. A new friend suggested doing an online party and she offered to host.

Olivia decided it would be a good thing to make masks for our family. She was a bit scared of all the virus talk and wanted to be sure she and the people she loved had some protection.

The only challenge for me was grocery shopping. I took

advantage of the early morning senior hours (it was a bit tough to be told I was in the at-risk older population age 65 and older) and was amazed by the empty shelves, little meat, and no toilet paper. I already did a lot of online shopping so I used that to get what we needed. Life wasn't much different except that I now had a child here five days a week and almost five nights a week.

I found myself as a long-term second grade substitute teacher, trying to follow the teachers' assignments and enhance the curriculum so there was a full day of school. I was cooking three meals a day most days (pre-COVID this meant a mid-morning breakfast, a late lunch around 2 with my husband, and then snacking later on). With a child here full-time, it was three meals plus multiple snacks in between. That meant I was constantly washing dishes too. It seemed I was getting much better acquainted with kitchen duties- duties that had lessened over the years.

Our classroom moved full-time into my studio. I was sharing my workspace all the time and it was getting messier and messier. It was not only a school room and jewelry studio, it became a mask making factory as I was churning out masks daily. People asked and I couldn't say no. I accepted orders via my website, using up small pieces of fabric, clearing out my stash. I'd ordered large rolls of elastic to keep up which was challenging in and of itself. I'd received substantial orders from non-profit organizations through close friends. Suddenly, I had made close to 200 masks and sewing them wasn't relaxing or fun any longer. My stress level was building.

Social media was booming. Invitations for events on all kinds of topics, from people I knew and liked, and I couldn't keep track of them.

I tried to be a good friend and actually attend these events until I couldn't any longer. Social media invaded my life. My stress level was building even more. I found I was getting irritated more often and not knowing how to fix it.

Then, tragedy struck our family. My husband's brother died in early April. His health had been failing and he was in a nursing home. He tested positive for COVID-19. It was not the cause of his death but a contributing factor to his body which was shutting down. We were faced with figuring out how to grieve in this new time when families couldn't come together, console one another, touch one another, cling to one another. It made the news reports of people dying alone even more real to us.

Seventeen days later, tragedy hit my husband's family again with the sudden death of his sister. He received a call that something had happened and as he readied himself to go to the hospital, a second call came in to say it was too late, that she had passed on. Again, his family had to figure out how to grieve.

That day, my son and daughter-in-law came to pick up Olivia so we could have a quiet house and I would be able to attend to my husband's grief. He was out when they came and after they left, the house was quiet. I sat in my chair and realized that for the first time in a couple of months, I had the house all to myself, in all its silence and I could just breathe. I felt free of any responsibility. I only needed to pay attention to myself.

Resentment and anger were building. I wanted my life back. My refuge, my quiet, was gone. My social media time was bombarded with noise as all of us entrepreneurs were trying to pivot our businesses in this new world order. Groups popped up everywhere, invitations to join multiplied and guilt was setting in if I didn't accept. As much as I like to keep busy, I found resentment growing so much so that I just wanted to quit everything.

I didn't want to be in groups. I didn't want to have to track what group was having sessions when. I didn't want to do Zoom networking. I didn't want to make any more masks. I didn't want to be a teacher. I didn't want to cook every day. I wanted my life back as I knew it. And I felt guilty.

COVID ISN'T GOING ANYWHERE. Schools remained closed through June. A new rhythm of the weekday evolved with school beginning by 9:30, completing assigned work and enhancing the curriculum with other resources. The studio became our favorite place to be where we both could work across from one another and I could help her when it was needed. She was becoming more self-directed. By two in the afternoon, the school day was over and Olivia found projects to do to keep her busy and creative.

Shopping for groceries was still challenging. In mid-May, I scored on a shopping trip to the grocery store and stocked up on meat. I felt giddy with delight and couldn't wait to tell my husband. The same day, my husband brought me flowers for Mother's Day plus a package of toilet paper! Who knew I would be rejoicing over meat and toilet paper, things I had taken for granted all of my life.

Social distancing had become a reality of this new life. Zoom socializing was the only way to see my friends and family. I used Zoom to socialize with close friends and my sister in California and her husband. It was better than a phone call because we could see them.

I'd also been able to get all my siblings and many of our children together to celebrate my mom's ninety-first birthday via Zoom. She was able to see all her children and several grandchildren. While it wasn't the best session with technical difficulties, the idea that we were all together for the first time in years was amazing since we are spread out across the country in Connecticut, California, North Carolina, New York, Washington, Maine, and Nevada. Now with this new platform, we could have a family gathering.

I continued making masks (over 400 in total), but in a more relaxed way. I learned to say no if it would become too much. Mask-making brought in some income that allowed me to pay for my book illustrator and not take the cost out of my daily budget. I didn't want to be an opportunist, but COVID gave me an opportunity to make a little extra cash which I could use towards the outlay for my book.

Work on my book seemed to be progressing. I'd found an illustrator who created adorable watercolor drawings that matched my vision for the book. My book was going to become a reality. I started my author Facebook page to begin promoting the book's coming to be able to sell copies and recoup my expenses and maybe, even make some income. But then the illustrator missed his deadline and stopped responding to my inquiries after I'd received a few of the drawings. Feeling defeated, I contacted the freelance service which determined my order should be cancelled and thankfully returned my money. This was much more work than I'd realized and I decided to reach out to the publisher that initially accepted the book who set a team in motion to work with me to make it a reality. It was going to cost more but reduce my stress in making this dream a reality.

I returned to yoga and meditating on an almost daily basis. Amazingly, this simple practice helped me begin to count my blessings, the first being that the time I was having with Olivia was the biggest blessing in my life. Who would have thought that I would have this much time with her, to get to know her even better, to teach and to influence her and give her memories that will last her lifetime, to know that one day she will share her story of COVID-19 and tell her grandchildren about her time with Nana and Papa. I realized that so many grandparents weren't able to spend time with their grandchildren at all and I had her five days a week. I was grateful. I thanked the universe for giving me this great blessing.

What was interesting is that once I recognized that blessing, so many others came forward. I'd made connections with women so I wasn't lonely. We could have one-to-one sessions, chat, and support each other. One new friend hosted my first ever virtual jewelry party which was an astounding success! This was going to be part of my new business model as a way to broaden my reach, connect to women who wanted my jewelry, and to better understand my customer. I was reaching my 2020 business goal of getting known but in a different way.

Even though I opted out of several groups, I did keep up in the group coaching sessions. As we all shared how we were feeling and how we were being impacted while we were trying to maintain momentum to propel forward, we all were feeling much the same – sadness, loneliness, apathy, frustration, grief. A part of me was ready to just shut down, hide out, give up on my business venture.

Our coach is wonderful for hearing the core of what we all say and sharing her wisdom that causes us to think and reflect. She encouraged us to find our compass point, to prioritize what was really important and what really mattered. I was told to embrace the fact that everything is not fine and that I am not okay all the time, that it is in times of "not-okay" that clarity can set in. It is times of "not-okay" that growth can occur, that change can be made towards becoming okay.

POSTSCRIPT–THE NEW NORMAL? As June came in, a new rhythm of life emerged. I listened more to what others were feeling, to what was going on in the world, to how people's lives were changing.

A different kind of gratitude and happiness emerged for me. I began to assimilate various lessons I'd learned over the years in how to create, and live, a simplified life, filled with who and what matters, leaving everything else behind. My stress level has declined to near non-existent and joy has returned.

The wisdom, for me, from this time of COVID is simple:

Spend time with those you love. If they are close by, make the time from your busy life to be with them, enjoy their company. If they are far, talk to them, do video chats, do more than like their social media posts and comment back and forth. Be personal with those you love best.

Clear out the clutter. In your home, in your closet, in your social media lists, in your life, in your mind. Clutter just stresses us out and we need far less than we think. Find a coach if you need to who can help you declutter. You'll find what's left is what really matters and gives you joy.

Prioritize. The world you knew may come back and you have thought about the things you like better. More time with family. Family dinners. TV nights together. The word I heard frequently was "together". Define and keep your boundaries. No job position is worth losing these intimate moments that are priceless.

It's okay to treat yourself to life's little guilty pleasures. It might be a glass of wine, a piece of chocolate, your favorite pizza or pasta, fresh caught lobster, rich and creamy ice cream. Indulge once in a while–there's no need to deny yourself all the time. Yes, you're focused on building better health but I firmly believe there is room for indulgence too.

Revel in the beauty around you. Smell the flowers, watch the clouds move across the sky (maybe even lay in the grass and look up at the sky to see what shapes the clouds are), smell the fresh air, put your feet in the ocean or sand, nurture plants, gasp at the gorgeous sunsets.

Lastly, give thanks to whoever or whatever you believe in. The universe has given you a life and it is up to you to determine how you will live it. Give gratitude for the little things which really, in the end, are the big things.

Namaste.

ABOUT APRIL

April Goff Brown is a Connecticut native, retired from a career in youth services, and now relishing this stage of her journey through creative ventures. A self-proclaimed "creative-preneur," April designs and crafts natural stone and sea glass jewelry as well as memory quilts and landscape quilts. She is completing an illustrated children's book based on an experience with one of her granddaughters. She is happily married to her husband of 40 years, proud mother to her son Jason, stepmom to April, mother-in-law to Cori, and nana to seven. She has also been adopted by Iran, her son-in-love.

A recent (two year) convert to yoga and meditation, April has been awakened to the universe and its many blessings of close friendships and family, and a strong network of fellow women entrepreneurs. She counts among her greatest blessings having her granddaughter Olivia with her during this pandemic, and is grateful for the joy she has brought each day.

Website: www.aprilbjewelry.com

"The universe has given you a life and it is up to you to determine how you will live it."

APRIL GOFF BROWN

Connecticut, United States

CHAPTER 10

Hidden Blessings

GINA RAPOSA JOHNSON

The landscape of business looks very different than it did at the start of 2020. There is no doubt the COVID-19 pandemic has hit small businesses hard. As a business coach working with entrepreneurs, I can tell you first hand the challenges were real. Many of my clients felt blindsided as the world began to pause.

My situation was different. I have always worked from my home office, and so, personally, my business hasn't changed all that much. But I knew I needed to pivot as my clients' needs were changing. As times grew more uncertain, not everyone was comfortable investing and committing to a three or six-month coaching package.

After conducting a "SWOT" Analysis of my business, I discovered that I needed to have a low-end package offering. I created a brand new signature package that includes a 90-minute coaching session with a personalized "SWOT" Analysis. It's the right fit for my clients—the package is flying off the virtual shelf! Adapting my business to meet the needs of my clients was the model I knew I needed to coach my entrepreneurs on. Over the last three months, my clients have had to both pause and accelerate a few creative changes in their businesses. Pre-COVID-19, the majority of them generated revenue from in-person services. Now it was becoming increasingly clear that it was critical for them to pivot in the uncertain environment.

It was...just survival mode for everyone.

When I spoke with my clients I asked the tough questions: "What are you going to do? What are the decisions you need to make right now to save your business?" For those with a brick-and-mortar location it was about making choices so that they could successfully reopen when the crisis was over. For others it was about changing their offerings to meet their customers where they are in the moment.

As the weeks and months went by I was astonished by the hidden blessings my clients uncovered as they shifted their businesses.

Laura Giro, a Spiritual Development Teacher and owner of Alba Energy and Spiritual Development, transitioned from in-person meditation classes to virtual classes online, which actually doubled her attendance. Her students loved not having to commute so much and now Laura is offering daily online meditations. She is using the meditation sessions to grow her YouTube channel.

Laura says, "The current situation allowed me to have more time alone with my daughter, which I love! I've had time to dive into figuring out what my life's purpose is, what is true for ME, and removing the confusing "noise" of life that was standing in my way."

Jessica Mand, a Communications Professional and Founder of InDemand Communications, was no longer able to network and connect with her clients in real life, which she knew was crucial in helping them communicate their message across to their customers.

Jessica states, "When the pandemic struck a moment (or three) of panic creeped in. I didn't know if my business would survive. As I pivoted to online meetings and Zoom calls, quickly learning the meaning of "Zoom Fatigue". But after the initial flurry to accustom myself to a flurry of online activity and repeated eye-strain, I learned to recommit to a sustainable work-life balance."

"With more time at home, I learned just how important exercise is to maintain my mental health. I created a gym on the carpet right in front of my fireplace. I learned to recognize when I was starting to burn out and how to quietly excuse myself from the fast-paced online rat race to go quietly meditate. I figured out how to find calm in the COVID-19 chaos."

Licensed Massage Therapist Christy Arnott, owner of The Holistic Connection, made the difficult decision to close her brick-and-mortar practice after being open for just 1 year.

Christy shared, "I was devastated that I was no longer able to help my clients in their healing journey in-person. Massage therapy was such an important part of my mission to care for others. I didn't know how I was going to continue that level of care."

"Closing my physical location actually opened up my schedule to help a greater number of people instead of just one-on-one interaction. I decided to expand my reach by returning to the corporate world, but this time working for a company that aligned with my wellness values. By embracing the extra time I now have I have refocused my efforts on writing medical-grade meditations for a digital health and wellness company, whose mission is to partner with hospitals and clinics around the country to integrate meditation into the current healthcare system. My new role means I have a greater reach helping people heal. I never could have imagined the blessing in the crisis."

These are just three of the many success stories my clients have had. Each client has a new sense of excitement, reigniting the passion back into their business. Scaling my business back-to-basics to meet their needs has also renewed MY passion. Everyone has been so appreciative of the help I've been able to offer them.

It has become the spark to remind me why I decided to start my business–to help others reach their highest potential.

I have had a positive personal outcome from the pandemic.

COVID-19 has really changed my daily life. As an extrovert by nature, I was pleasantly surprised by how well I adapted to the isolation of our stay-at-home orders. I really love the home bubble that I have created. From spending time out on my deck to spending more time in the kitchen, I've really embraced being home. My newest joy is afternoon bike rides. My hidden blessing has been the gift of connection. The pandemic allowed me time to slow down and spend more time with those I love. There is no greater gift!

About Gina

Gina is a Holistic Business Coach, Mentor, Marketing Guru, and Reiki Master, guiding her clients through powerful proven marketing, branding and business strategies. She is an accomplished Motivational Speaker, Workshop Facilitator and Retreat Leader. As an Entrepreneurial Business Consultant and Business Mentor she connects 'people to people.'

Gina specializes in working with entrepreneurs and start-ups to develop strategies for acquiring new business, establishing their niche and creating signature offerings and packages.

Gina sits on the Board of Directors for Caritas Smile. She travels abroad with the non-profit organization to help rebuild villages in remote areas while helping to create life-changing moments for people. She is the Chief of Staff for Cloud 9 Online, a digital health and wellness company specializing in Medical Grade Meditations. She is on the leadership team for eWomen International.

Website: www.ginajohnson.co

"There is no doubt the coronavirus pandemic has hit small businesses hard."

Gina Raposa Johnson

Connecticut, United States

CHAPTER 11

Dream

JACQUELINE A. BALDWIN

We have the choice as to what lens through which we view this pandemic. We could feel like victims or become beneficiaries of COVID-19. It is true we all have been forced into isolation. No hugs, no going out to meet friends for drinks, no school, no work, no 5:00 a.m. yoga class, no church. Our hair is either in desperate need of TLC or has been completely shaved off (just going by the three men in my house). The world has come to an abrupt halt.

In the earliest days of "social distancing," fear and panic ensued. The herd mentality caused us to hoard all manner of items including toilet paper of all things! I couldn't even find one stinkin' roll of single ply. I was forced to ration the precious rolls we had and interrogate my fellow housemates as to their daily usage as I saw empty cardboard rolls accumulating in the trash can. And yes, at one point things became so desperate we had to resort to using up the napkins before I could find a single four pack on a shelf. It got so bad I had friends on the hunt for me from other towns notifying me of a fresh delivery at their local store! The shortage led opportunists to take advantage of those of us who failed to plan ahead, making a buck off of the fear mongering by selling toilet paper, hand sanitizer, much needed masks at highly exaggerated prices. While an average cost per pre-pandemic roll of toilet paper was $0.84 there were reports of single rolls being sold online for nearly $15!!! That is a 1,800% price increase. This takes supply and demand to a whole new level!

The streets became eerily desolate, no one out walking dogs, no children riding bikes, no loud annoying cars in need of a new muffler to jar the silence. The feeling that if you even opened your door to the outside world you were taking your life in your hands. Going to the grocery store meant arming yourself with a mask, gloves, and sanitizer wipes. I found myself driving through parking lots assessing the danger before eventually venturing out into the virus laden battle ground.

As a financial advisor, I watched in disbelief as the stock and bond markets plummeted in record fashion. The Dow Jones Industrial Average had its worst one-day point drop on March 16, 2020 of 2,997 points. The S & P 500 plunged a shocking 26% in only 16 trading sessions. Paychecks ceased, retirement accounts were evaporating, savings accounts were non-existent. Was this the end of the world? Should we be reaching out to our loved ones and telling them how much we cherish them?

I remember distinctly the moment I made the choice to stop living in complete fear and to embrace this once in a lifetime moment where we all get to take a breather without fear of missing out (FOMO).

I had been glued to the news. Watching as New York City, a place I absolutely love, was under siege. Makeshift hospitals were being set up throughout the city to accommodate the overwhelming numbers of infected people. The counters showing COVID-19 cases, hospitalizations and deaths were visible on every electronic device I own as a constant reminder. I spent Easter Sunday sobbing, grieving all I had lost! I tried to find solace at my favorite hiking spot–no luck. I thought maybe if I worked really hard outside until I was ready to drop I would feel invigorated–nada. I finally cried myself to sleep feeling alone and defeated.

That is when the shift happened.

I woke up and decided that, if in fact this was the end, then I was not about to spend it lying down. It was time for me to take my power back. I got dressed (in my business attire–no leggings!), sat at my desk, put a timer on for myself that would literally close Facebook for the day after 30 minutes of engagement, and got to work! I made phone calls checking on family, clients, acquaintances determined to put a smile on their face before the call was over. I started DOING for others instead of wallowing in my loss and that shift in energy started shifting the energy of those around me. It was a powerful reminder to me to be a mirror for what I wish to see. The good in my life needs to begin with ME. I found myself embracing the isolation. It gave me time to be with myself. Marinating in what used to be opening the door to dreams of a magnificent life yet to be.

The Great Pause known as the COVID-19 Pandemic, has given in the taking. The go-go pace of our lives has come to a screeching halt. It dawned on me that this time for us is like a yellow caution flag is for NASCAR drivers. Everyone must hold their current positions, no passing to get ahead. The drivers take this opportunity to refuel, get fresh tires, rest for a few seconds. While they certainly want to finish the race, this pause from the deep concentration required when traveling 200 mph is a much-needed break, allowing them to clear their minds and refocus.

For those of us non-essential workers, this time has provided space for deep connection with those we love as well as with ourselves. Families actually sit down, perhaps even at the dining room table, and eat dinner together, play games, work on puzzles. Zoom, a virtual room, entered our vocabulary. Zoom happy hours have replaced going out. No need to get a babysitter! Who would have thought virtual game nights with distant family members would become a regular event? Families across the globe have reported that this pause has strengthened their bond which had been weakened.

They say necessity is the mother of all inventions and my, oh my, has this pandemic gotten the creative juices flowing. One such invention was a new way to create beautiful music "together" while being apart. Musicians from all over the globe have been able to come together on one screen and produce one magically melded sound for the world to enjoy. This certainly has exemplified the hashtag #WeAreAllInThisTogether. For a brief millisecond our country and I dare say the world was unified in a battle against this invisible enemy.

I have been reminded of the stories about World War II that my parents would share. They talked about how automakers stopped making cars and started building tanks, airplanes and even helmets. In this pandemic wartime automakers have pivoted to making life saving ventilators. Not only has this ability to innovate provide a critical weapon against the virus, it has kept many Americans employed. Other manufacturers, such as my brother's company, shifted from making paper products temporarily to making personal protection equipment keeping medical staff faced with daily exposure to COVID-19 safe.

Hotels were suddenly shuttered. They have become makeshift hospitals, shelter for the homeless, places for doctors, nurses and EMTs to stay between grueling shifts in order to not bring the deadly virus home to their loved ones.

Churches have turned to online services reaching those, who may not have stepped into a church otherwise, a place to go to find answers and comfort through faith.

In addition to virtual get togethers via technology, the car parade has been born! Teachers drive through their students' neighborhood reassuring the younger students especially, that everyone is still really out there beyond the confines of their home. Friends and family drive by horns honking, signs stuck on cars, balloons dancing out windows to celebrate a birthday, graduation, birth of a baby.

For the huggers of the world, months of not holding one another has been excruciating! In order to provide some relief to that pain, hugging through plastic walls with arms allow some grandparents to once again share their love with their grandchildren. Human touch is said to boost our immune system and reduce diseases such as those associated with the heart. We certainly could use that today more than ever!

Suddenly we find ourselves with plenty of time for introspection. For some, like me, being alone has forced me to really dig deep into my soul. With nowhere to run and hide, my past traumas that have been plaguing me for my whole life were free to come out of the dark. With far less distractions, the guidance of a great coach, along with a deepening faith I decided to once and for all meet these demons head on, refusing to allow them to go back into the back of the closet only to come out whenever they desire to sabotage me.

I had the space I needed to do the work! At long last I have been freed from the bondage these ugly experiences kept me in! Self-doubt, unworthiness, and paralyzing fear have all been kicked out of the house for good! Pleasant dreams and restful sleep have been restored.

"The Impossible Dream (The Quest)" from the musical *Man of La Mancha* (composed by Mitch Leigh, with lyrics written by Joe Darion) challenges us to reach for the stars and dream the impossible dream.

Throughout this crazy and unique time in our world's history there has been tremendous sorrow and destruction. But out of the ashes a rebirth is happening.

The planet Earth itself is having its own moment of healing. In only three months, we are seeing meaningful signs of Earth repairing itself all across the globe. Waterways such as the Venice canals are clearing. Air quality is improving as harmful emissions are reduced due to lessened consumerism. Wildlife is photographed roaming free, bringing signs of hope to a hopeless time. If every person made a conscious effort to do at least one thing a day to conserve and preserve, imagine how much better the earth would be.

I see improvement to our overall physical health. Getting back to basics, of growing our own food, eating less processed food, exercising, getting more rest will all have a lasting effect on the quality and quantity of life. Reform of our current healthcare system has been born out of necessity during this period of "stay safe, stay home." Telemedicine along with other pivots in healthcare due to social distancing have actually had unexpected benefits. While the telehealth systems have been available for nearly forty years, many consumers and physicians have been reluctant to utilize them. When forced to, they are actually finding that outcomes are improving and costs are being reduced.

Will we be tempted to return to pre-pandemic habits? Will families begin to get back on the treadmill of life, running children to activities, working long hours, grabbing fast food to scarf down before scooting off to the next event? I believe we will long for those simpler days and make intentional choices to recapture at least a bit of that simpler life. I see a world full of passionate people today, refusing to be complacent about the injustices that abound. I see creative minds seeking innovative ways to problem solve life's quandaries. I see today's youth teaching their elders what it means to be resilient as they navigate their new not so normal.

So may the kitchen dance parties continue, the Zooming keep connecting. May your toilet paper holders always be full. May we continue to extend a generous hand (not physically of course unless it is gloved) to our brothers and sisters no matter the color, whether it be big or small, wrinkled, calloused, well-manicured, or lacking digits.

We have a responsibility as well as the ability to make this planet a better place. We have witnessed first hand the destruction that we humans can impart in every manner to the world around us. We have also witnessed the very best humanity has to offer. Earth has been nicknamed the Goldilocks planet. As in the fairy tale of Goldilocks and The Three Bears where the young girl named Goldilocks wants everything to be 'Just Right', Earth is thought to be just right for its inhabitants. We have managed to bring the only habitable planet to the brink of destruction. This is our chance to restore her to her nickname.

So together let's dare to dream the impossible dream!

About Jackie

As a financial advisor, Jackie is passionate about eradicating financial vulnerability.

Her specialty is advising women who feel financially unprepared for the big what if's in life so they can feel confident knowing they have solutions for weathering any kind of storm.

Jackie felt financially vulnerable throughout her former marriage. After years of being kept in the dark, the dreadful state of the marital finances was fully revealed during the divorce process. Jackie vowed that she never wanted to feel that level of vulnerability again. From this experience, her desire to help others to feel safe, secure and enlightened was born.

Great confidence comes from knowing that with Jackie's guidance, her clients can not only survive the great what if's in life that come their way including economic challenges, they *can* thrive and experience a vibrant future.

"For the huggers of the world, months of not holding one another has been excruciating!"

JACQUELINE BALDWIN

Connecticut, United States

Coming Home

stillness

first steps

time

love

CHAPTER 12

Sitting Still for a Guy Diagnosed with ADHD with a Nickname of Do-Do-Davidson

DAVIDSON HANG

As someone who is always on the go, COVID-19 taught me to see the value in being able to take time for myself to rest and relax.

I work at LinkedIn, volunteer for more than six different NGOs (Streetwise Partners, IMentor, Exploring Paths, Orphans Future Alliance, and many off events) and overall I would say I live a very fulfilled life. I am a social butterfly, hosting many of my other events such as happy hours, fundraising, I am a part of Linkedin's Wellness Champions, on the board of Cheers for Charity, co-lead at LinkedIn's Asian Alliance, Toastmasters at Microsoft and Linkedin, and love attending all of the meditation, mindfulness workshops, and leadership and development seminars.

When others put time on my calendar they say they have anxiety just taking a look at it. My mantra was 'sleep is for the weak' and that people who say we need 7-8 hours of sleep every day to be fully functional is a lie. I thrived on 5-6 hours of sleep every night, and I was out to prove people wrong.

Some of my favorite things to do and bucket list items revolve around traveling, meeting new people, hosting events, and being in large crowds like EDM events at festivals. These things source me.

I've done enough personal development programs to know what helps me get into a slow state and what doesn't. I once did a meditation all day retreat and it was the hardest thing in the world for me. My happy place is doing an 8-hour Spartan Beast up a mountain in Killington, Vermont or Mt.Vernon.

I was once told that I was the most extraverted person they have ever met in their lives. I would agree. I've been to over 1,000 networking events, BNI, Toastmasters, seminars, and being an outside sales representative I have taken advantage of as many free, high-end happy hours as possible. I have networked my way through my career and I have loved every minute of it.

In the Accomplishment Coaching training program, my constant restless state earned me the nickname of "Do Do Davidson." The program taught us that the state of being is more valuable in many instances than the state of doing-because it is who we are being that others see in ourselves.

Now that you understand the context you can see why COVID-19 was extremely challenging for me. My world was flipped upside down. No more waking at 5:30am to do Crossfit! No more going about my day conquering the world ahead of me!

The beauty in this pandemic is that the scariest thing in the world for me is to do nothing and just sit at home. And it forced me to do just that.

I spent my entire life running away from home, living at everyone's homes but my own. I am not sure why it was so hard for me to stay home. So imagine now living 3 months with another person's family when you value freedom, adventure, exploration.

What was I running away from? Was family really that bad? What about my mother and father could I not be with?

When you have hundreds of hours sitting alone in your room (well, technically, in my fiancée's parents' guest room) you find out a lot about yourself. In giving yourself space you learn more about yourself. I've learned more about myself and who I am in these past

3 months than I ever have in any other 3 month period.

When I sit in silence, I find peace and tranquility amidst the chaos. I find that I am the sole person responsible for my life. I cannot blame the economy and society. What I've learned about myself and others is that whatever is coming up during this pandemic is actually what we have been running away from our whole lives.

Was sitting in silence the worst thing in the world? Maybe for a guy who runs 20k every day according to my fitness tracker or someone who thrives on being able to see a thousand people at work and love every minute of it. We often are attracted to what we perceive we did not get during our childhood and teenage years. For me surrounding myself with ambitious go-getters was what I thought I did not get with my parents.

In these moments, I started to realize how much my mom and, yes, even my dad cared about us. Yes, they were probably not the most fiscally responsible people in the world, evidenced by the fact that we never owned a home before or that we moved around as much as we did. Was my father escaping reality or having to deal with unpaid loans? Was I doing the same by ignoring the fact that my true love was right beside me? Why did I have to go out, conquer the world, make new friends, and add to my ridiculous Linkedin connections count?

One of the most memorable moments during COVID was when I reached out to many of my good friends who are all really far away from each other.

We started doing Zoom calls and my friend Jameson said, "Man, it took a pandemic for all of us to hang out again." They are all successful people as well being nurses, pharmacists, and doctors in Philadelphia, the Bay Area, Southern California, and me being in NYC.

I started calling my good friends whom I was too busy to hang out with because I was busy saving the world one immigrant, one high school/college student at a time. Don't get me wrong, I've still been able to volunteer and do many of the things that I love but I've never tapped into my creative juices as much as I am right now. I'm so proud of myself because the scariest thing is creating a video and rewatching myself.

The opportunities and blessings that I have seen is that there is no barrier of distance now. I'm fortunate to work at Linkedin in the Empire State Building where I work with some of the greatest minds in the world. There are a thousand of us at Linkedin programming to stimulate any interest I have whether it's learning something about social impact, diversity, inclusion or belonging, or if I want to do a yoga class.

We often strive to get promoted, sacrificing family time, and getting back at unreasonable hours. Those in the Northeast United States especially can relate, most of my days looked like getting up at 5:30am and coming back home at 11pm. You would think I am exaggerated but I am not. Honestly, I am not even sure how my fiancée puts up with me. There were so many days where she said I just want to be able to cook dinner with you or bake something together. Can you also include me in your plans or at least ask me before you commit to a 16-week volunteer commitment?

We are finally starting to communicate with each other. Staying home together for three months will do that for you! I am finally starting to see the value of taking it easy and family has always been a complicated topic for me. Growing up, I did not have my father most of my life. He just left one day without telling us why, how, or what was happening. It traumatized me and at the same time was probably the best thing that has ever happened to me.

It's a complex question, but I do realize that if it wasn't for this time of isolation and my fiancee and her family's risk tolerance, I do think I would still be roaming around filling up my days with things to do because it looks good on paper.

I was able to pursue many of my passion projects that I was scared shitless to work on before. Working on a book is nerve-wracking for someone who barely passed English, who always scored very low in the verbal and the written portions of the SATs, and pretty much any standardized test. The only writing I had under my belt was as a sports editor in the school newspaper.

I had started my YouTube channel and my podcast a few months ago, but was inconsistent. These have finally started to come into themselves after I was not "allowed" to go out anymore. Every time someone gave me feedback I made excuses like, "I don't have time to learn how to video edit or edit my podcast." Those excuses no longer existed.

When I sat with myself for hundreds of hours I started to realize how glad I am that I wasn't born in Vietnam where maybe the opportunities are not as plentiful as being born in the U.S.

I'm fortunate that my mother immigrated here as a refugee escaping the Vietnam world. She told us everyday growing up how lucky we were that I got more than one shoe or that I didn't have to work seven days a week. Growing up wasn't easy for us. I hated how much I had to work to pay for my extra expenses like going out with friends while most of my friends didn't start working until after college. By the time college happened, I had had over ten jobs and side hustles. Life was not fair and why was I so unfortunate to have had such a rough upbringing?

Perhaps, sitting alone in my own thoughts isn't so bad after all. It led me here: to writing this book, to sharing with you.

What Future Do I Dare to Dream Of?

I dream of a workforce where managers do not need to micromanage us. They trust that we adults and human beings are capable of succeeding without having to punch a clock or having to be told what to do and how to be our best selves.

I dream of a place where we do not have to watch the polar caps melt.

What if humans actually related to each other as one instead of what religion, color, what school you went to, how your accent sounds, or if you believe in a different god? What if no one is right and that everyone's opinions matter the same? Not because you are a rich, middle-to-later-year white male who went to an Ivy League School and was born in America, the UK, or any European country?

Man, these moments really allow us to appreciate walking across the Brooklyn Bridge, the day I can do that without a mask, without avoiding people like they have the plague or even worse the coronavirus. NYC restaurants have always been a highlight of my life, being lucky enough to have such amazing experiences with so many loved ones and friends, coworkers, and family.

Hiking mountains and being outdoors sources me. Humans naturally from thousands of years of evolution want to explore and we are social creatures, the chances of survival were much higher when you were in your tribe. I get that we all might not share the same opinions, parents growing up, and upbringing. I do know that humans are social beings at their core and even people who claim they do not like people are lying to themselves. They just don't want to admit that they actually really want to be loved and embraced.

I was one of those people who had to meet people to see how this one person can benefit and add to my life. Upon reflection and time to myself, I realize that I am not perfect and I have so much more to experience in life. I am grateful for this pandemic to help me realize that relationships matter and I've created a bucket list of places I want to travel and visit. I get to appreciate all of this so much more when it's all over and done with.

About Davidson

Davidson is an Account Executive at Linkedin Learning Solutions. He is a YouTuber, Blogger, Podcaster, Public Speaking Motivational Coach, and mentor.

Davidson's life's purpose is to create Curiosity, Reflection, and Abundance. He helps others see the humanity in themselves by helping people find a purposeful drive so that they are happy, fulfilled, and radiant joy. Passionate about social impact, making a difference, and helping others foster a sense of diversity, inclusion, and belonging, Davidson's goal in life is to be able to help others find peace.

Davidson thanks his therapists, Accomplishment Coaching, Landmark, and NextLevel Training for their healing work, which has helped him inspire and touch thousands of lives annually.

Website: www.davidsonhang.com

"What I've learned about myself and others is that whatever is coming up during this pandemic is actually what we have been running away from our whole lives."

Davidson Hang

Manhattan, New York City, New York, United States

CHAPTER 13

Not So Little Things

ANNAMARIE WELLINGTON

John Lennon sang, "Life is what happens to you while you're busy making other plans." When I stop and reflect on the experience of living through the COVID-19 pandemic, it becomes clear that Lennon's words resonate far beyond his short lifetime.

I wear many hats in my daily life. I am the Director of Education at a higher education trade school where I am the boss to a staff of twenty. I am the administrator students come to see when they are in trouble, when they cannot handle their own lives, and when their burdens are just too much to bear alone. I am a graduate student who is finishing her dissertation. I am a friend who supports and lifts up others to help them achieve their potential. I am a daughter, a sister, an aunt, a cousin. I am a wife. Of all the titles I hold, the one I hold closest to my heart is the simplest one: I am a mom.

I have two beautiful children: Liam, who is six and Elie, who is thirteen months. My two babies are my pride, my joy, my heart, and life. Liam is a very vibrant, energetic child with a mischievous streak that clearly was inherited from me. He is also a kind, gentle soul who wants to take care of everyone around him. He loves nothing more than snuggles and hugs. He is smart, loves math, and exhibits a curiosity about the world around him. Elie is my fighter. She was born six weeks early weighing in at four pounds, eleven ounces, and proceeded to spend over two weeks in the NICU at Greenwich Hospital before she had the strength to venture out of the hospital and come home to join her family. She has spent more than her fair share of time being sick and has had trips to Yale

University Children's Hospital during her very short life, but she continually proves she will not be beat and keeps her sunny disposition no matter what happens.

This school year was the start of many new adventures for my Liam. We moved to a new house in a new town last July, so he was going to be starting a new school with new friends and a new teacher. Liam has a big heart and wears it on his sleeve, so there were many nights leading up to the start of the school year where Liam woke in the middle of the night worried whether or not he would make new friends or if his teacher would be nice, would he know how to buy hot lunch on pizza day or where to go to the bathroom if he needed it. I promised him that he would love his new school and that this would be his best school year yet. How little did I know when I made that promise what was in store for all of us.

Working in higher education, I was acutely aware very early on how the COVID-19 pandemic began to impact the day-to-day lives of people in Connecticut. Our school started participating in weekly then daily calls with our corporate office as well as various officials from the state to discuss what would need to change, how our process would need to shift, and what the pandemic would mean if it were to spread. While actively trying to plan for the welfare of my student body and my employees who look to me for guidance, all that consumed my mind was the wellbeing of my precious babies. As the pandemic continued to spread and our school was forced to move to distance learning, I knew I had two very distinct roles I would have to manage: one as Annie, the Director of Education and supervisor; the other as Mommy, who had to protect her babies and make sure they both continued to learn and thrive while learning and developing at home.

When schools began to close and the shift became one to distance learning, I felt that as an educator, I thought doing distance learning with Liam would be a breeze. I was basically running the online learning of a whole school—how difficult could first grade really be? Little did I know my special guy would teach me as much about being a teacher as I would teach him about math, reading, phonics, writing, and science. What I had not planned to teach him was that life is full of unpredictability, heartaches, and frustrations; but that out of these challenges can grow love, compassion, and joy.

We spent our mornings sitting across the dining room table from one another, each on a laptop working. I was checking in with instructors and answering student emails; Liam was working on addition and phonics. We took coffee and hot cocoa breaks together and I listened to what he was learning through his Google classroom sessions with his teacher. We talked about how seeds grow, the different sounds vowels can make, and why we capitalize certain letters. I listened as Liam talked through how to add single digit numbers to make two digit numbers, and how to add two digit numbers by grouping tens and ones. I listened when he got frustrated and yelled that he wanted his teacher because she explained better than Mommy. I held him and hugged him when he cried because he missed sitting on the carpet to listen to the day's story time with his friends from school. When he asked questions about the coronavirus and why everyone had to stay home, I tried to explain it in the most simple terms I could without scaring him. I was amazed when he listened, thought about it, then came back to me a few days later and said, "People need to just save their own germs to keep everyone out of the hospital so no one else gets sick." It was fascinating to watch how his six-year-old mind made sense of this unchartered territory that so many adults were having a difficult time processing.

As a mom, I was proud to see Liam's compassionate side emerge while we were sheltering-in-place at home. He began to talk to me and my husband about the people we knew who lived by themselves and how they might be lonely. After finishing his school work each day, he would get out his arts and crafts bin. The first couple days I was angry at the mess of construction paper bits, markers without caps, and glue sticks all over the family room.

When he came to me with a pile of completed art projects and asked for envelopes to mail them to everyone he had thought of that might be lonely or would like a picture, my heart melted. His favorite person to send mail to became his great grandmother who lives in upstate New York. Liam loves his GiGi, and he explained to my husband and me that he wanted to decorate her house with pictures to make her happy because no one could visit her so she didn't catch germs. It was beautiful to watch him carefully practice writing her letters, drawing her pictures, then folding them into a large yellow envelope, then addressing it to mail to her once a week. She was overjoyed to receive his packages and called him every week to thank him and talk about the pictures he drew.

When the pandemic began and masks were required for going into public places, I began sewing. After sitting and watching me make masks, Liam asked me to show him how to help make masks. He was excited to try the sewing machine and learn how to make something to help other people. He was proud to finish them and send them to his grandparents and his GiGi. He wanted to help take care of the people he loves. I continue to beam with pride at the compassion that my young son is learning in thinking about others and their needs before himself.

As a mom with a full-time professional career, one of the things that has torn me apart since Liam was born has been needing to leave them in the care of other people to go to work. I constantly experience feelings of guilt as to whether or not I am doing what is best for my children by having other people care for them. During this pandemic, I have been afforded the opportunity to watch my precious baby girl grow and develop.

I went back to work when Elie was four months old and missed several of her firsts—when she first sat up, when she began crawling, when she first held her own bottle. When the pandemic began and I was afforded the time to be home with my children, I got to watch Elie try different foods for the first time, say her first words, stand up on her own for the first time, and most recently take her first little steps. I have watched her silly, happy personality develop with her little giggles, head twists, and claps when she succeeds at a task she tries to master. I have been able to watch how she sticks her little tongue out of the corner of her mouth when she is focusing on something, just like her brother does and like my mom did when she was focused on a task. I have been grateful to see her learn how to communicate her needs and wants while also learning how to play on her own as well as with her brother, her dad, and me.

During these three months of being sequestered at home, I have watched my daughter explore her world and develop communication and movement skills. She has started speaking in short words and sounds to indicate what she wants. She clearly has her daddy wrapped around her little pinkie—she calls "dada" and he comes. She also knows she is funny; her whole belly laughs with her bright blue eyes and blonde curls light up the room. Elie has learned to stand up on her chubby little legs and start taking steps. She was holding every piece of furniture and hand she could get for the longest time, but finally has let go and taken a few steps on her own. She falls down into an eruption of giggles every time she loses her balance. She is a bright light shining through the darkness of what is happening in the world.

The greatest joy the pandemic has brought me has been my children having time together that they would not have otherwise had. Liam greets his sister good morning every day and sits with her to eat breakfast where he talks to her about what he wants to do that day. She babbles back, and he talks back to her as though he understands. They play together, laugh together, and snuggle together. When I have virtual meetings to attend, Liam volunteers to read to Elie or to sit and play with her while I am busy. He often will lay on the floor and let her climb all over him, only to wrap his arms around her in a bear hug and give her kisses. The day Elie was born and Liam first met her, he nicknamed her "Elie Bean" because he said she was as tiny as a jelly bean. He now calls her "Bean" as his nickname for her. One of Elie's first words was "Um" which is what she calls Liam. She looks for him when he is not in the room and calls him when she wants him to come play. Liam has undying affection for his little sister and loves to snuggle with her. While so many in this world spent the quarantine time being angry about not being able to leave their homes and being inconvenienced by having their children underfoot, I am thankful to be able to watch them grow and see the love and friendship developing between them.

With the many roles I fulfill on a daily basis, the pandemic has given me the opportunity to slow down, take a deep breath, and look at my life through a different lens. I have been given an opportunity to spend time with my family while still fulfilling my professional goals. I have been given the chance to love my children unconditionally; if that meant taking a break in the middle of the work day for a game of Sorry! with Liam or playing peek-a-boo while getting some food into Elie, then I took the opportunity to do so. While my hours spent on my work computer were later than I would have done in person, the breaks to enjoy my family have been a treasured escape from the everyday career concerns. I have been able to spend more solid time with my husband during the day over the last three months than I have been able to in the ten years we have been together.

Being able to shut the uncertainty of the COVID-19 pandemic outside our house and just be has been quite the welcome change. I had not realized before the pandemic began how badly I needed to take a step back from the daily grind of my life, but I now treasure the time I get to spend just fulfilling each role individually, with being Mommy my favorite responsibility of all.

Growing up my mom always told me, "Everything happens for a reason and when it's meant to be." I never understood the sentiment until I was an adult. Shortly before I got married, my mom was diagnosed with cancer. We rejoiced when she was able to come to my wedding and were thrilled when the doctors shared with us that the treatment she was undergoing was working.

Three months after I got married, Hurricane Sandy happened. I was living on the beach with my new husband at the time, and we were flooded out of our home. We went and stayed with my parents for ten days. Every morning we got up, my mom made us breakfast and packed us a lunch to take while we went to our condo and dealt with the damage and the clean up. After a week and a half, we were finally able to go home. We packed up our stuff, I thanked my parents, and we headed home. I called my mom when I got home—she always wanted to know we got in safely—and thanked her again because we really didn't know what else we would have done had they not been able and willing to take us in.

That night, my mom passed away. I will always be grateful that I had those last ten days to spend with her: getting back at night and sitting to talk over a cup of coffee; sharing stories she hadn't told me before about when she got married and when my siblings and I were born; seeing my mom as a woman who had given up so much and endured so much to raise four children, yet wouldn't hesitate to do it all over again. Sandy gave me that time to be with my mom one last time and I will forever remember that my home being flooded led to some of the greatest memories I had with her.

I feel the same sense of peace and joy that came out of spending the last days of my mom's life with her as we are starting to come out of this COVID-19 lockdown. While I don't know what the future will hold with the resurgence of this disease and how it will potentially impact my life in the future, I am thankful that I was given three months of time with my children that I would not have had otherwise. I have gotten the opportunity to watch my son grow out of his baby face and childish behaviors and start discovering who he wants to be as a person. I have gotten to spend time working with him as a student trying to get through first grade, but also as a mom teaching him life lessons that he might have learned through school or through the aftercare program because I would have been at work. I have been able to watch Elie's personality emerge and see her start to come into her own. I have been able to be a part of watching her silly personality and funny expressions light up a room and warm her brother's heart. I have gotten to experience her inquisitiveness and see her make sense of the world around her while her brother teaches her through his example and playing with her.

More than anything, I have gotten to watch my children love each other. At the end of the day when they go to bed and I curl up with my husband to watch a show before bed, I can rest knowing I have been able to keep my family home and protect them from harm, at least for now.

About Annie

Annie has worked in education for seventeen years, including as an English teacher at Bridgeport's Central High School, the Assistant Principal for Academics at Trinity Catholic High School in Stamford, and currently serves as a Director of Education for Lincoln Technical Institute. Annie holds Bachelor of Arts degrees in English and Theatre from Central Connecticut State University; a Master of Arts in Curriculum and Instruction from Fairfield University; Certificates of Advanced Studies in Educational Leadership from Sacred Heart University and in Catholic School Leadership from Creighton University; and is currently completing her Doctorate of Education from Northeastern University. Annie prides herself on being a loving mom to her children, Liam and Elie. She and her husband Michael look forward to continuing their family travel adventures once COVID ends.

"I am thankful that I was given three months of time with my children that I would not have had otherwise...More than anything, I've gotten to watch my children love each other."

Annamarie Wellington

Connecticut, United States

CHAPTER 14

This Time. This COVID Time.

CAREN PAULING

To say we were burning the candle at both ends is putting it mildly.

We are a pretty typical, American, busy family of four. And when I say busy, I mean BUSY. Husband working long hours. Kids with multiple activities that require constant driving around, dropping off, picking up. When the calendar was so full and my goal was simply to keep us all alive through the busiest season, I slapped 2 hot dogs on two hamburger buns (because it was all we had), wrangled my kids into the car (with their "dinner") and drove to yet another lacrosse game scheduled inconveniently at 6 p.m., requiring me to drive through Hartford rush hour traffic to get there for 5 p.m. warmup.

We were alive, but hardly thriving. This is just one example of how busy our lives had become. It was a constant battle to get from one place to the next. Our family was a foursome of ships passing through the night, with barely any room to breathe in the chaos.

I'm not saying I don't love the activities that have become a central part of our lives. I love my athletic, teenage son who thrives on sweaty practices, 5:20 a.m. ice time, and late night varsity hockey games. I love watching him do what he does so well, what makes his heart sing. I love the hockey families we have known since these kids started skating. And I love how God made my son to love this stuff. I love what makes him tick.

I adore my sweet daughter and her cello lessons, her youth group, and Girl Scout events. Saturday mornings for the past few years have consisted of orchestra and chamber rehearsals for her, Starbucks runs and errands for me. I cherish her friendships. I adore the back and forth conversations amid carpooling to catch up with the girls who have blessed our hearts for years.

I just hate the busyness. I have always said that I was born into the wrong era. Is it wrong or backwards to admit that I look back with embarrassing fondness on my life growing up in the seventies and eighties? When spring and summer meant spur of the moment mustering of neighbor kids for kickball games, setting up my lawn chair for a day of baby oil tanning (burning) in my backyard. Days spent climbing trees with a paperback in my back pocket and reading in a branch for hours? If it is wrong to long for these days, then I admit my guilt! When I look back on those years, I never, ever remember running around to multiple activities without a second to breathe and really thrive.

That's what I've loved about this time. This COVID time. This slowing down of life. This recognition of all that matters.

Oh, don't get me wrong, I never want to "love" a time where others are suffering, in pain, in worry, or stress. My heart cries for the deaths of young and old, victims of this ugly virus. More than that, I hurt for those who are fearing and anxious. That's absolutely not what I love about this time. I don't love that essential workers have put their lives on the line to fight this battle. While I'm not gripped with fear over the virus, I still vigilantly don my mask. I disinfect. I go about the business of protecting myself and my family. That's not what I'm loving about this time, this COVID time.

I just love that life has slowed down. And I believe that's part of God's plan for this time, these months, for such a generation as ours. In the grief, and the fear, and the unknown, there is a gift to us. A gift that many of us have remembered if we've been around long enough to remember a time when we just weren't so busy. That's the gift.

As my husband transitioned to work from home, and the kids to online school, all the people I love most under our one roof, I find myself back to the simpler days that I cherish. I find more quiet time (some of this occurred as I've literally been "shushed" a few times by the teenagers as they take to their personal classrooms/bedrooms). So I sit in my bed with my coffee. I recognize a deep breath I needed to take, at that moment. I appreciate that deep breath because it's something I hadn't noticed doing much of before. I take more time with the God I love and who loves me, who desires time with me. I read His Word more. I pray more. Because I have more time. Time with God is not scheduled in between rounds of laundry and errands. It's deeply important to me. It always has been. But now, I can be face to face even more with my Creator, because I literally have nothing else to distract me.

Psalm 51:12 (NIV) says, "Restore to me the joy of your salvation and grant me a willing spirit, to sustain me." I've often struggled with this verse, especially the part about a "willing spirit." My struggle is having a spirit that shakes off the noise and clutter of this world and fully relents to a God who desires an unhindered relationship with me. God doesn't want the last yawning moments of my day. No. My God doesn't desire "my hot dog on a hamburger bun" attempt at relationship. He wants me quiet before him. Distractions set aside. My focus. My willing spirit. My spirit intentional, breathing deeply, loving well, and fully. My spirit, fully present and given without hesitation to the people I love, under my roof. This time, this COVID time, has changed me into a woman who doesn't just desire more time with God but literally craves it.

As the weather changes to spring and I am once again relegated to my bedroom while the others work quietly in their own spaces, I open my window and listen to birds I've not taken notice of before. I watch a fox daily walk past, just strutting down the street most mornings, sometimes with a squirrel or a chipmunk in his mouth. When I don't see him, it's actually strange, because he walks by at nearly the same hour, every day at 10 a.m. Once, in early May, we were surprised by snow. I saw the same fox and just marvelled at how beautifully red his fur was against the white background God had painted that morning. How I marvel at my great God and His creation! These are things that were always going on around me. It was me, distracted ME, who failed to see them and enjoy them. Now I have time, this COVID time, to truly delight in them. I have a willing spirit.

Relationships strengthened with neighbors who have more time to walk, en route to our nearby bike path. We're not merely waving now and getting back to our garden work. We're stopping and talking. Talking about the real stuff in our lives, our real fears. My goal is to bless them and know them better. Conversations with our backyard neighbor, Patty, who just lost her father. Hearing her love for him, her memories of him. She apologizes for getting emotional, but God loves the transparency when we can do life with the people He surrounds us with. Recognizing that she needed an ear, God placed her in my path to simply listen. He has purpose for me in this. I'm learning to listen to His voice whisper where He needs me.

The blessing of a bread machine and how my family scarfs down a French loaf I remove from it. It's gone within minutes! Sharing a loaf with a fairly new neighbor I'm still getting to know. She then comes over and blesses me reciprocally with a sack of flour I needed because the store was out. This is beautiful. This is exactly how God wants us to love our neighbors.

This life, this COVID life, has brought people together. My church family connects over Zoom. Even the older folks in choir with me. We have time to listen to each other just... share. We pray together. We mute ourselves and sing "together" along with a video our director plays. I've loved these people in person and I love them even more now because we're doing life together in a different way.

Now we can't really rehearse, so we simply take turns sharing. When they share their daily lives I feel literal pain that I can't give a precious older lady a hug, because her back is hurting and she feels anguish. I had taken hugs for granted. Help her, Jesus!

I see this time, this COVID time, as a time of intention. How can I love my family more? What can I recognize God doing in my community? How do I see Him more in the everyday stuff I've been too busy to really even see, for years?

This slowing down has allowed me to see the world not unlike the world I lived in as a child and teenager. When we stayed home. When our activities didn't unhinge us. I remove leaves from underneath the rhododendrons in front of my dining room window, and I remember the rhododendron from my childhood home that we had our prom pictures taken in front of. The garden my Dad tended to that produced the most delicious Burpee tomatoes that we ate freshly sliced with Italian dressing. I can still taste the iced tea we'd make with fresh mint from the garden. I tend my own perennial gardens and get the soil under my fingernails and marvel at how good it feels. Amazing garden hormones are released. Yes, it's a thing! Gardening as therapy and memories of gardening giving me peace. God wants us to notice and love these things. My willing spirit is the reciprocation of His incredible gifts to me. I'd still be gardening without COVID, yes. But gardening more slowly, enjoying God's presence while working. That's what's different. That's what's precious. When I'm a grandmother someday, I'd love for my own kids to share memories of our home like I have of my own childhood home and garden.

Two and half months into this time, this COVID time, our world breaks in a huge way with the death of George Floyd. I am forced to confront my own heart issues regarding justice in a way that will change me forever. Had we not had COVID, had we been in our busy time, I would have scrolled more quickly through my newsfeed. I would not have taken the time to pray for God to break my heart for all the things that break His. I would previously have treated my heart issues with a quick slap of a bandaid. Now, they needed examining. I needed to be tested. I needed to confront these very things in a conversation with God that will be ongoing. His timing is perfect.

A friend asks me when we'll ever return to "normal?" As we slowly begin phasing back into "normal" I actually have a heart response that surprises me. The truth is that I actually enjoy this. I enjoy this time. This COVID time. I like the pace of it. I like hunkering down. I like slowing down. And if I'm really honest, I'm not so sure I want "normal" again. For I have a willing spirit now. I am changed. I want to be changed for the people in my life who already know me well and the people I hope God brings into my life to know better.

And while I desperately want this virus to go away, the life that it gave birth to, this COVID life? I think I'll be ok with it sticking around for a while longer.

About Caren

Caren Pauling enjoys the blessing of life in beautiful Avon, Connecticut, along with husband Bill and teens, Danny and Meghan. When not tackling a fun short story, she enjoys running or taking long walks, endless house projects, substitute teaching, hanging out with her church's middle school youth group, and Chipotle take out. Caren dedicates this piece to the many neighbors and friends who have strolled past her window during this COVID time, including the red fox who daily trotted by at 10 a.m., giving her multiple opportunities to celebrate the beauty of all God has created.

"That's what I've loved about this time.
This COVID time. This slowing down of life.
This recognition of all that matters."

Caren Pauling

Connecticut, United States

Chapter 15

We Are One

Kathleen Troy

"your grief for what you have lost lifts a mirror up to where you are bravely working.

expecting the worst, you look instead

here's the joyful face you've been wanting to see.

your hand opens and closes, and opens and closes.

if it were always a fist or always stretched open, you would be paralyzed.

your deepest presence is in every small

contracting and expanding,

the two as beautifully balanced

and coordinated as birds' wings."

Rumi 13th-century Persian/Sufi poet

We saw it coming. Not unlike a swell of tide-in the distance you cannot tell if it is the "big" wave until it is nearly upon you. It either washes over you and rolls you onto shore, bathing suit filled with broken shells and privates somehow loaded with sand. Or you body surf it-feeling the churning beneath your stomach, and the power of a force beyond you. The shocking part of this is to realize that either outcome can and has occurred. We have been rolled. We have risen from the white lather victorious. We learned this the first time we played in the ocean surf. And we know the miracle of it all is that the water we experienced is connected to other continents far from view.

I suppose this image best explains my experience of the *Extraordinary Pause*. I share this as March 15-my last day of my Other Life has since rolled into June 5-summer has sprung nearly unnoticed by many.

I am aware that anything could have happened. My 30-year-old firstborn, Jameyla, called me two weeks into lockdown, and shared an urgent message. She lives in Tempe, Arizona, and still adorably calls me Mommy.

"I had a nightmare that we were all walking together at our old house in Bedford Hills. A car came from nowhere and killed you, Papa, and Sofia instantly." She awoke sobbing and horrified/relieved. "And you need to know. If anything happens to all of you, I will be devastated. But you need to know that I will be ok."

I did need to know this. I have had the same conversation with my parents. We need to know that our adult children can survive and have coping mechanisms. Never did it feel so relevant before this moment.

These are the awarenesses that have cropped up in this moment. Two nights prior to her dream, I had a sleepless night as I realized that everyone I loved, my whole orbit, could be vulnerable to this COVID-19 death. My elderly parents in Michigan, who resent that classification and continued to rebel unmasked and unfettered into April. My youngest who has type 1 diabetes and had hunkered down a little too late. My husband, Tt, who is such a germaphobe that I worry he has built too little immunity. Me. The "extra"

142

extrovert who was in tremendous contact with world travelers in my salon life/networking circle. I am a hair colorist/life coach who is inching toward coaching and turning my color life into my side hustle.

March 15, 2020- I visit Sofia and Kenyon, her germaphobe boyfriend. We socially distance, and he sprays me (with permission) with alcohol when I sneeze. That evening my friend Keith calls to say he is not feeling well. I was with him March 12 in NYC as Broadway shows were about to close. Paranoia sets in.

March 16, 2020- My older ladies, 80+ years old, are the last to brave the public realm. "If I die of this thing-I am not going to my grave looking like this!" Staff and clients awkwardly circle each other. Cancellations-phone ringing off the hook at the salon. The stress is palpable. Women crying as college students book flights to return from study abroad. Travel plans cancelled. Random frightening reports of COVID positive patients reported in surrounding communities.

March 17, 2020- I woke up as a 56-year-old. After a sleepless night I realize that the only way to stop the madness is to stop showing up at the salon. I commit to a life of integrity. I know now that my friend Keith, who I saw recently, truly feels awful. I ask my employer to stop too and close the salon. He chooses to wait.

March 25, 2020- I am going to have to find a system-waking and sleeping off schedule makes the days run together. I know that at this pace, the shutdown will be a blur. I commit to more than a blurred existence.

March 30, 2020- I search for humor. Silly memes. Facebook groups of quarantine humor. Comedians. Musicians. I am grateful and my mood shifts to gratitude for these clever strangers. I continue calling people I know to be alone. My elders actually support me and my resolve to be a comfort, not a burden, strengthens.

April 10, 2020- My Tt continues to find new vacant parks and trails for us to explore. A bit of green reveals itself. Spring is upon us. Rainy. Colder than March. Peaceful.

It took a couple of weeks to find a pace. I had not had a span of unstructured time since I was 15 years old. I do not include six week maternity leaves or one month leave for surgery on a fractured hip as such.

I have to set the alarm for 5:30 a.m. to meditate and stretch and to feel on top of my day.

I took my own advice-and designed a joyous, productive, flexible schedule.

News remains dire. NYC epicenter. Heart-wrenching losses. Lonely deaths. Lonely nursing home patients. Isolation shines a harsh light on our crumbling systems. Bodies pile up in refrigerator trucks.

April 20, 2020- We reminisce and celebrate how well our daughters are navigating this upheaval. I reflect on when my husband rose as optimistic family leader years ago. We had a house fire at 2 am. We escaped without sleepy 5 and 8 year-old girls in tow. The firemen swarmed everywhere. I told Tt that I am sad for the girls for this traumatic experience. "Oh, no! This is a gift from God! We are given an opportunity to role model for them in the face of challenge." He is exactly this way right now. How we all benefitted.

May 1, 2020- Cuomo remains a powerful, compassionate voice. Trump remains ridiculous. I vacillate between pouring over news and avoiding it at all cost. My forever optimistic husband asks me to stop sharing these reports. I am clouding his day. He is correct.

Yoga 3-4 times a week. Zoom video networking and Discovery sessions. Zoom fatigue. I was not cut out for office work or working from home. I must find stronger structures. Sixty-five percent score for fitbit step challenge-and that is generous.

May 7, 2020- My gong arrives! It has been on my Vision Board and I always imagine situations call for a gong. I miss gong baths. I miss kundalini yoga in a studio.

I finished my full moon kundalini yoga class on the Flower Moon in Scorpio. I am still dressed in white at 9:30 pm when my door chimes sounded. I thought my guy Tt was locked out. Peeking through shades, I saw a Fedex truck and the driver holding a huge box. "Sorry to deliver so late!'

"Oh no! You are right on time!" I know in my heart that my husband conspired with the moon to give this to me. He always thinks I am odd, but somehow he knew the joy this would bring to me. Swoon!

May 30, 2020- We took a walk on this splendid morning. This is our routine. The lilacs have reminded me for weeks that breathing deeply is rewarded. How wise to have given us these remedial and glorious reminders. Another miracle. Tt cannot be in the presence of our robustly fragrant lilac trees and manage to speak all at once. He agrees to buy and plant some with me. He avoided gardening until now-and it is heart melting to choose plants together and measure their new hole placement as one.

Last night I co-hosted our first *Holding Space* event with my very dear Beth and Jane. We have created a weekly Zoom event to be available and vulnerable with people in our lives who may benefit from deep breathing and community.

Hearts have shredded these last few weeks. Such losses and grief. News that causes heart palpitations and fear. Acts of love, solidarity and beautiful musicians sharing their talents freely with the public have also been created. There is so much to take in, and so much time to do so.

We ask for an emotional barometer-an anecdotal scale of 1-10. Participants, over the weeks, begin to trust that they can be at a 2 (barely out of bed) or declare a 10 and feel no guilt for experiencing joy in the company of devastation. And realizing that we may all be up and down the scale any hour of a day. The measuring system brings solace.

Most of my inner circle are united in believing this is a new beginning. The Age of Aquarius is now. Our souls chose this incarnation and have secret knowledge of how we will exit this scene. We conspire to generate critical mass of love and healing vibrations. The task, at times, seems herculean. And there is comfort in processing this period as we go, rather than having it trip us mysteriously months after. This is our intention.

From this place, I am able to practice gratitude. I thank the COVID-19 victims for their soul sacrifice in showing us all the holes in the swiss cheese of our society. The lack of care for our most vulnerable. The lack of respect. The magnified love and heroics of so many helpers-essential workers and angel medical staff who have come to save and comfort so many!

June 2, 2020- On the docket: going to the dentist for my cracked tooth. I have moved this appointment three times at the urging of the nurse. "If you are in pain, keep your appointment. If not, shall we move it for a month?"

I also refuse to have my thyroid checked. "Please just fill my prescription one more time!"

Tt is also our grocery runner. I go out for nothing but hikes.

I think I may have crossed over to the antisocial, hypersensitive, shut-in personality. I am not unnerved by this awareness.

I am more paranoid because my husband is panicked about all exposure opportunities. He is certain that I will return as a silent killer. The "curve" has dissipated, yet there is still a fear of unknowing. To remain in absolute alert avoidance, then to submerge into closed public areas, evokes many emotions. We learn that his sister has had a heart attack and his brother and wife have COVID-19. They are in Pakistan and they are all so feeble. I share his panic. These are the in-laws who present as patriarchs and matriarchs of the family. I married the youngest brother, and I am much younger than all of them. I love them so much and feel his grief. They accepted me into the family so lovingly.

I suddenly realize what this entire period has revealed to me!

My husband and I quit our jobs as young newlyweds and spent three months living with my in-laws and having wild, dangerous, gorgeous road trips throughout untamed Pakistan. I returned to the states with such regret-I wanted to live in Lahore and rear our children with all the bright, engaging, loving cousins. I loved how I felt there. The food, the feminine salwar chemise. Women seemed more like colorful flowers.

We returned pregnant, jobless, money spent, and feeling irresponsible. I wax nostalgic as I remember the love. And I honor how brave we have been-and responsible-ever since.

Thirty-one years ago-and I am more in touch with that three month sojourn than ever. That was the last time we spent any extended amount of time together. I look at him and feel the same best friend adventure buddy soulmate feeling as I did at the base of the Himalayas. Deep, deep gratitude makes my breath falter. He is still so delicious and handsome. Kind and forgiving. The years melt away, and I am with the kindred soul that swept me away just yesterday. I lovingly called him an enigma-and still do. I knew it would keep things interesting if I could not figure him out. This has also been our challenge.

Tt colors my hair for me. He claims that this is his third round and he demands to be paid for his expertise. My tooth hurts. I do not want to be cranky. He made my favorite lentils and he is coloring my stripy white roots. I try to remember what he gains from this relationship. I can think of nothing at this moment.

June 3, 2020- Sofia, my younger daughter, currently 26, and I have been wanting to collaborate on a workshop.

Two different desires intersected. I saw millennials isolating and taking on less than stellar self-care habits. Even Jameyla, who invited me to fitbit challenges, was allowing me to win the week step challenge. This is my competitive daughter. Something was not right. Young people I was coaching spoke of conditions of malaise, anxiety, and fear of an unknown future. Many were the most pragmatic about shut-down rules. Initially, Zoom happy hours and connections were sought after. As weeks dragged into months, they were losing steam. I wanted to serve them and connect them all. Create a new conversation where they were not alone.

Breonna Taylor. Ahmed Aubrey. George Flynn. The COVID threat paled as demonstrators took to the streets.

He is scared. He asks me not to protest. Exposure. Violence. It is too much for him. Perhaps for the first time in our marriage, I comply. We agree to donate to worthy causes and to find other ways to support our black community. My heart yearns to be in solidarity with the peaceful protestors.

Sofia and I had already booked a workshop to bring her friends together. "Mommy. Can we talk about racial injustice? We just cannot ignore it. There is no way to connect and not address it. My friends are devastated." She also insisted that we do not make it about Millenials. My daughter called me out for my exclusivity, and wanted to include all ages. I complied.

So we pivoted. We chose Black Visions Collective as our cause the first night.

June 4, 2020- We had an amazing turnout. I asked some of my nonwhite friends to join us specifically to guide us and weigh in on how this could go. I teared up as I saw friends of Sofia's and mine pop in. Jameyla in Arizona even shifted her lunch break to participate.

We all agreed to do this weekly. Sometimes awkward, not completely smooth as a workshop-at least Sofia and I admitted that these participants are our beta-testers. She led breathing, heart-opening, and throat-opening mudras. Proud, very. What was present-hunger for these conversations. There is a compulsion to open up, be vulnerable, and to learn how to have these taboo conversations out in our circles. We have a collective desire to learn how to remove vocabulary that is inherently racist. We desire tools to challenge racists in our circles from a place of "What makes you say/feel that way?"

An opportunity for growth-we only had one man. My friend said, "Why am I always the only man?" He is the most likely to show up everywhere for the things I invite him to. My friend, an older Haitian doctor, thanked us later. She exclaimed, "Imagine if groups like this form across the land!" Yes. Imagine!

My husband creates a vortex of his own joy. He is doing no harm and loves his introversion. He cares for me and shows me every day what love and consideration feels like. He maintains that racism is not as prevalent as I think. Times when I see a hairy eyeball staring at him, he believes that I am looking for trouble. That I distinguish what I want to see. He simply refuses to take anything personally. He lives The Law of Attraction, having never read it. He embodies the Four Agreements, having never studied them. Do you know how frustrating it is to live with Buddha? He will not be joining our weekly workshop.

June 4, 2020- We received word that salons open next week. June 9th in Westchester. This is in the midst of riots and increased numbers of COVID cases. This is weeks after we adjusted to no longer being the working class. This is as a gorgeous summer unfurls. Most of us have been inside for years. Missing the beautiful sunshine. I personally have never felt better physically. Yoga 3-4 times weekly with Sofia via Zoom. Hikes. Meditation. Writing. Creating a vortex mostly filled with light-except when I tap into news and dig deeper. I feel the tug of reality. My sleep is off now for days with nocturnal anxiety.

My husband is concerned. "What is going on? Can you wait to go back and see how it goes?" He senses my mood shifting. Is it duty and obligation? Avoidance of messy endings? Missing the connections to my beloved clients?

This loop is like a tilt-a-whirl ride at a carnival. My guy stays with the ride, chirping in here and there. "We could do this if we continue not to spend." I know me. I will spend again.

"Is it even safe? Can you wait a few months?" Not sustainable in this business. You snooze. You lose. No way do I have the energy to rebuild a clientele. Not in the beauty industry.

Meanwhile, the country is burning. Racism, misunderstanding, fever pitch divide has never been at this level. And COVID marches on.

And we are safe in our vortex. I love my vortex. I am so in love with my husband. May I stay here?

Where is here? The love that was always available from my partner. I spent so many years noticing the differences, that I came close to missing the gifts.

I have often mused that my husband and I have only these things in common- two daughters, a taste for lemon, and a sense of humor. I was wrong. We have so many nuances that fit and expanded over time. And I see so clearly that marriage is a consistent "choosing in." It is dynamic, not static, when we allow for different rates of growth. Partnership was available, when I did not shut him out/down. He is very sensitive, and I can tread hard.

Between us, I still want to be more like him. His easy access to joy. His brilliant mind. His efficient habits and ability to complete near impossible tasks without a complaint. His skills and talents that span many areas of concentration. He is musical, too. A Pakistani Renaissance man.

The pride I feel when I make him laugh heartily. The extraordinary kinship when we laugh hysterically with each other is contagious. I feel the kindness in his inability to utter a harsh word -ever.

I remember how my mother cringed when I told her early on that I had found my guru in him. I now understand that he is a version of myself that I continue to strive to experience.

This man, who I initially rejected as 'Too Handsome' (an active bias way back when), raised an ocean and world of traditions apart is so uniquely the only man for me. And he is the perfect playmate in a pandemic. Who knew? I send love back over the span of time to my young self. I thank her for following her heart, and for taking a leap of faith with this mysterious, exotic man.

I commit to keeping this precious lesson in the forefront. I will reread this every month to stay in this lesson. And most of all, I wish for all of us to understand the gifts available in expanding our universe to include people of very different backgrounds. Your life will be exponentially enriched.

About Kathleen

After many successful years in the NYC beauty industry, and rearing two daughters with her husband, Kathleen Troy became an ICF certified Ontological Life Coach. She graduated from a rigorous National Coach training program held in NYC, Accomplishment Coaching, and accessed her deeper purpose through this process.

Kathleen enjoys facilitating personal development workshops for small businesses, corporations and collectives, yoga retreats in partnership with yoga specialists, and individual coaching sessions. She was invited to facilitate a Women's Empowerment Session at the U.N. and was deeply moved by the powerful, vibrant women in attendance. Every person matters.

Website: www.secondspringcoaching.com

"The years melt away, and I am with the kindred soul that swept me away just yesterday."

Kathleen Troy

Connecticut, United States

Being Human

adventure

healing

acceptance

trust

thrive

CHAPTER 16

A Time for Green Waffles: A Meditation on Life in Urban France

MARY ANN WATERMAN

It was Friday evening of our final day of school, for a really long time. I went with Sasha at the end of our day to the bar OzArcades in Place Saint Louis. OzArcades had been the first place I ordered a beer when I had just barely arrived in Metz. The owner kindly asked in German, "Ein Beir?", after I struggled for "biere", in French.

School had been cancelled indefinitely. It seemed as though we were on the precipice of a wild new adventure. That afternoon, in our Directrice's office, my colleagues were feeling nervous. The conversation had several times spun out into despair. While certain facts were unchangeable: we would likely be out of school until after the spring holiday in early May, we would receive technical unemployment-a French invention where we receive pay because we cannot work due to factors beyond our control, we were far from alone in this novel situation.

As I would often do on a Friday, with my daughter, Sasha, we went out for some food. Another favorite of ours was the Roman style Pizzeria, Nonna. A little pizza Romana and a glass of rosé always seemed a perfect way to accelerate the transition into the weekend.

We ordered from the menu of café classics. Sasha had a Croque Monsieur, the spectacular grilled ham and cheese with a layer of cream cheese and an extra layer of melted cheese on top. I had a

Tartine, topped with spicy mayonnaise, pulled chicken, and onions. "Tartine" literally means to spread on bread.

As it happened, there was live music that evening at the OzArcades. A French singer with a guitar was performing some traditional songs. We listened to several "Chanson Francaise," as we slowly took in the atmosphere. People were gathered at tables inside. The light was fading at 18h30 as we waited for our dinner. Even though we did not know that the restaurants and bars would be closed from midnight the following day, in this café, populated mostly by those forty-sixty years old, there was a sense of appreciation for the ambiance that was provided that evening.

***

The sheep, a beautiful mixture of brown and white, are grazing on the hillside by the Parc Seille. They have been enjoying the grass for some time now. I do not know when the sheep arrived. It was sometime during our deep lockdown, when our radius of travel was limited to one kilometer. The Parc Seille is a ten minute walk from my apartment.

What does it mean to travel only one kilometer from one's home, the initial restriction we had in France? When I had lived in Alaró, Spain, on the island of Mallorca, Palma, a twenty minute drive to the coast, was considered far. We had discovered that in our small village, populated by an interesting mix of locals and expats, heavy on traditions, and entrepreneurs, we were not often drawn to leave our little oasis.

***

We have returned to school now, but, with many precautions put in place. The children's tables are spaced one meter apart. We are highly organized. My French colleague and I have been taking turns, one day cleaning each material, then, the next day presenting lessons to the children. The parents remain outside of the classroom. The children enter by themselves to set up their tasks for the day, as is customary in a Montessori environment.

In early June we are able to travel in France again, but not more than 100 kilometers (about fifty miles). I think of the once radical 100 mile diet. What is behind these initiatives? The Fundamental Needs of Humans in Montessori Elementary curriculum categorizes human "needs" according to necessity. As I recently explained to Sasha, we actually need very little. Sure, there is a natural imperative to decorate ourselves, and, when the essential needs are satisfied, to create culture. Our needs are actually quite simple, though: food, clothing, shelter.

Last night, gathered with a large group of friends at home for the first time since March, we opened one of the literal 'fruits' of our labors: sweet pomegranate infused vodka. After having discovered a cast off cocktail bar sign early on in the lockdown, I told my boyfriend Dany that we should open a secret bar featuring interestingly prepared concoctions.

***

In the initial week of the French lockdown, or, as we would say "Quarantine", translated from Italian to mean forty days, the streets of Metz were very quiet, but, also somehow familiar to me. In August, the mandatory holiday month in much of Europe, for the two weeks after the celebrations of the patron Sant Roc, everything is closed in Alarò, Spain, our former village. This closure, on Mallorca, and, in other parts of Spain especially, is seen as a necessary pause after such chaos as a week's long party entails.

The first two weeks of quarantine, in Metz, we had many days when we would plan our time entirely around the recipes we found in Dany's two cookbooks. One book, titled *Tart*, was filled with delicious warm combinations that oozed strong French cheeses such as rustic Camembert. The other, a healthy approach to interesting recipes was heavy on the zucchini. We hand grated several zucchini on Saint Patrick's Day to make our green waffles.

***

During the first week in May, when stores, and, some schools, opened up, I had a sense of confusion at the sea of shoppers. In the Grand Est, which was still a "red" zone at the time we did not yet have access to parks and gardens. Who were these people who could not wait to get back to buying things to put in their white shopping bags? Macron, the President was encouraging such behavior, as an Economist.

Germany has Merkel, the physicist. Ireland, a doctor. Which country is run by a philosopher? I wonder if as the whole world we have had this "Great Pause", that we must, on some level, emerge changed. I think this time is a form of meditation, for those who vibrate on a level to take note of it. For me, going back to work, to society as such, I take comfort in those moments of peace. Of my quiet walks around Metz when I only looked at the gargoyles.

I find myself drawn to new projects. With some friends we are starting a community theatre troupe here in Metz. Our first production will be on the 15th of July, the day after the usual Bastille Day festivities that this year have been cancelled due to limiting crowd size. For weeks I read the New York Times in its entirety from my open window. I took heart from Ben Brantley, the Theater critic, who recommended reading plays aloud in the living room. We will be American and Russian astronauts cooperating amidst the Cold War.

Today, there is impromptu live music in Place Saint Jacques. Set up outside, three musicians take turns serenading the crowd. I observe from the table of a nearby restaurant the concert from behind. The music is in French. It is a lively scene. And, there is the sun.

About Mary Ann

Mary Ann is originally from Thomaston, Connecticut. Mary Ann has her Bachelor of Arts in English from St. Joseph's University and her Masters in English Literature from Trinity University, with a specialization in metaphysical poetry. She is an Association Montessori International (AMI) trained Montessori educator for 3-6 year old children. Recently Mary Ann has been living in Metz, France with her nine year old daughter. Mary Ann loves learning new languages, creating recipes, and, following a serendipitous life path.

"I wonder if as the whole world we have had this 'Great Pause' that we must, on some level, emerge changed.

I think this time is a form of meditation, for those who vibrate on a level to take note of it."

Mary Ann Waterman

Metz, France

CHAPTER 17

Healing the Human Experience

Brittany Luna

Pandemics bring nothing but fear, trauma, economic destruction, and death. How could we ever look at something so devastating in a positive way?

While it's completely understandable to believe nothing good could come from a devastation such as COVID-19, this view keeps us stuck mentally, emotionally and spiritually—not just through a pandemic, but through other obstacles we face in life.

At the very least, the experience of COVID-19 has worked like a magical mirror; showing us things about ourselves that we might not have otherwise seen, including how we perceive the world and life's experiences. Personally, COVID-19 presented me with the ability to look within, or simply look around, and see truth; something we can all do should we choose to recognize it. I saw the truth about myself, my relationships, and the way I perceive the world.

Truth is not black and white, but every gradient of grey all at the same time. Truth allows us to hold space for all things without choosing one or the other.

Our Human Experience

Being human is fucking hard, a truth I certainly can't deny.

While that truth bears heaviness, it doesn't mean we have to make it harder on ourselves than it already is. If we didn't know in the "before time," COVID-19 continues to teach us that we truly have no control over the external world or others' behaviors or thoughts. It's brought us an uncomfortable awareness of more than we might be willing to attest to.

Awareness of our time, energy, and how we've been spending it throughout our lives.

Awareness of the things that actually mattered all this time, or didn't, and how much or little focus we gave it "before."

Awareness of rules and protocols that have been in place or needed to be, that were easily changed when push came to shove.

Awareness of the things we once felt we "had to do" being something we don't want to do anymore.

Awareness creates opportunity.

An opportunity to practice things we 'never had time for,' whether that's in the form of hobbies/crafts, meditation, or rest.

An opportunity to reconnect to loved ones, make phone calls, send texts, write letters or reconnect to the self, the soul, and our needs.

An opportunity to use our voice, to step up, to do what we can to help not just ourselves, but others' human experience.

An opportunity to start doing things we actually want to do, rather than the things others expect us to.

Why would we need to go through a devastating pandemic to create these opportunities for ourselves? Why would the universe do this to us?!

It's easy to look at COVID-19 as something happening "to us." It's easy to look at anything as happening "to us." It's the easier way to look at life.

Why should we have any accountability? Or in anything we perceive as negative? Why should we have to put in any effort to live a happy human life?

Have you ever truly learned anything about yourself by something not happening?

We learn through suffering. Our brain's main job is survival, so when something is seemingly threatening (like a pandemic), it's going to burn those memories into the mind to learn and grow from. To move through suffering, we have to be willing to experience suffering.

Humans outrun discomfort. It's a protective and learned mechanism of the brain-to remember the times we've felt uncomfortable and do what it can to keep us from feeling that again. Because who wants to feel like shit?

Trying to outrun discomfort is literally what keeps us uncomfortable. Our brain is going to work to find the opposite of what we're feeling, and if we can't "perceive" comfort, then the mind is going to continue to look for it, reminding us that we're uncomfortable.

A global pandemic, and all the fear it brings, isn't something we can outrun. We cannot escape the fact that there is a life-threatening virus out there. We cannot escape the fact that it's killing people around us every day. We cannot escape the fact that it's wreaked catastrophic havoc on our economy and our way of life. There are so many factors that leave us vulnerable and feeling out of control. But that's normal. It's normal because it's true.

We cannot control any aspect of this, nor can we outrun it.

It's also normal to feel anxiety or depression during this time as a response to that. We're surrounded by an experience that threatens our safety and security in our human meat sack in a multitude of ways.

But that doesn't mean we have to remain unwell.

Many people believe that in order to be "spiritual," or "enlightened," or to consider themselves "healed," that they no longer feel anxiety, sadness, fear, or have any "negative" response to life. They want to cut out the being human part.

You can't live a spiritual life without being human.

Being human is part of being spiritual. And being human includes experiencing every range of emotion, every high, every low, and learning how to navigate it. This starts by giving ourselves permission to feel the feels we are feeling; no questions asked. Cuddle up, get to know them, welcome them. That's how we begin to foster well being, whether it's literal depression, to simply feeling unwell; and not just during a pandemic, but always.

The beauty in COVID-19 is that so many finally gave way to the emotions they feel. Since all of us were going through it, it felt okay to finally freak out and let the feelings exist. We shared, we commiserated, we ruminated.

It's that ability to embrace the nasty that moves us out of a pandemic, *and* through life. We lived through a fucking pandemic. Food was scarce, human touch was nil, and uncertainty was everywhere. This is the LITERAL opposite of the appropriate environment for a human mind to "feel well."

Many experiences we have outside of COVID are also not conducive to feeling well. Yet, before this took an unhealthy route with our emotions, we'd suppress, deny, and shut them out until it became too much.

Perhaps one of the greatest lessons COVID-19 brought for our overall mental health and wellness was to simply acknowledge the feelings that kept us unwell. How we learn from this notion can shape our relationships with the self *and* others.

We've seen people at their absolute worst during COVID-19. Human beings were stripped of self-actualization goals to being a human attempting to survive. COVID-19 brought us zooming back down the ladder we were climbing toward "bettering ourselves" to "where the fuck am I going to get food?"

Some lost jobs. Some lost entire companies. Some lost homes. Some lost hobbies that helped fuel happiness, physical health, and mental health. All bringing us to that basic, primal energy that we've been fortunate and privileged enough to not only keep in the background, but build upon.

Being back in that headspace of just figuring out how to eat, get fresh air, keep ourselves sheltered, how to survive—creates the very basis of anxiety. My safety, my life, is threatened. Each one of us is going to process that differently.

Cultivating strong healthy relationships is a luxury humans have that comes only after ensuring our own basic survival. We've just never had to worry about that, let alone consider it.

Now here we sit in a relationship with two souls both figuring out how to survive—back to square one of being human. We might be constantly arguing because the stress is so overwhelming, we have no outlet, and the only people there to take it out on are one another.

While this might seem threatening to our relationships, it can actually be a gift, one that I most certainly am grateful for.

Relationships

When we've been in a relationship for a while, we fall into a rhythm. We have the way we speak to one another, the behaviors we exude, and even the energy that arises within that relationship. Relationships have a flow.

The beginning of a romantic relationship brings out the best in us. The other person is at the top of our priority list. Their happiness matters; and frankly, their happiness means our happiness means a happy relationship. We obviously aren't going to step into a brand-new relationship rearing our ugliest of moods at the get-go. We give it a little time before we scare the crap out of them.

But once that security sets in that "this person isn't going anywhere," that consideration we had might dwindle. Decisions become based on what's best for the couple.

This pandemic brought a powerful realization that we quickly forget that within a relationship lie two souls, living out their own life paths. We unionize those paths and consider them one; when in reality union is merely working toward similar goals for the family.

But those two differing paths still very much exist.

While I try to be mindful of my partner's energy as often as possible, quarantine brought a whole new level of need for this awareness.

Each person is still in there; working through their own lessons, experiencing being human in their own way, and figuring out what makes them happy as an individual. Being coupled simply means someone else is there for the ride.

The opportunity here is one to stop and remember what it was like at the beginning of our relationships–to consider the needs of our partner and where they might be at, understanding that they might process a situation like this much differently than we do, recognizing that their idea of their future may have crumbled.

Can we find it within ourselves to foster compassion, not only for our own predicament, but for theirs as well? Acknowledging that this isn't just about "us, as a couple" but them, as an individual. Every time I found myself annoyed or wanting to sulk in my own shit, I had to stop and remember that my partner, too, was struggling and that I could acknowledge that we both needed to experience our shit in the same small space.

If we can bring ourselves to this space, what could this mean for our relationship in the future?

Perhaps we learn to empathize with our partners state of being; something we may once have gotten annoyed by. Perhaps the things we once argued about don't seem as big anymore because we learned the importance of what really matters in life after being surrounded by the perils of a pandemic. Or maybe our communication skills shift because we're now in the same space for more than two to four hours at night before bed.

Whatever the realizations are, they will not come without the willingness to be open to compassion and empathy for both ourselves and for our partner, not just as a couple, but as individuals on their different paths. At the very least, we can reflect on how to best move forward in our relationships after a pandemic, regardless of what that means.

Understanding

Perception is quite literally the way we understand or are aware of something. Our perceptions are shaped based on our belief systems. What we believe, we will see. This isn't some magical adage trying to force you to believe why you should be optimistic. This boils down to how powerful your mind is; so powerful that it can literally change your physiology. Take psychosomatization for example; commonly experienced when someone has anxiety. If someone's fearful enough of having an illness, they can "psych" themselves out enough to actually experience the symptoms.

Beliefs extend far beyond the physical experience. They thread into our everyday lives. If we believe that nothing good ever happens for us or that we're "cursed," our awareness will be hyper-focused on the less favorable moments that make us lose our shit.

I call these "belt loop days." Have you ever attempted to walk out of your door and gotten the door knob stuck in your belt loop? You get yanked backwards, bash into the door, and scream, "FUCK! ARE YOU KIDDING ME? THIS DAY IS GOING JUST GREAT." Belt loop days.

These only seem to happen on bad days. Why? Because if we're already having "a bad day," our belief is that the day is bad and therefore, things that are simple annoyances are going to stand out strongly and "verify" we're having that bad day. We don't remember getting our belt loop stuck when it was a normal day because it didn't bother us. Our belief about that day, or our week, our life, or even a freaking pandemic, is going to shape what and how we experience it.

When we consider what experiences COVID-19 brought to the world, if your belief is that it only brought terror, trauma, and death, then that's your reality. If it's your belief that only bad things happen to you, that you'll never get ahead, or never "finally catch that break," then that's what's going to happen. Or at least it will appear as such.

What we believe, we will see.

The reality is, even if our dreams came true; the job, the partner, the money, we're not going to recognize it if that's not where our awareness is. Life will never change. Only you will. Your awareness is what changes.

Shitty things still happen. We lose loved ones. We get whacked with an unwanted bill. Our friendship is on the rocks. We have an argument with our significant other. We go through a pandemic. Life still happens. No matter how seemingly "perfect" it is for any one person. We cannot outrun being human or the lessons that go along with it but it's how we approach that experience that makes all the difference.

The belief that opportunities and positive experiences can still exist, despite them not going exactly the way we want, can create a powerful shift in our life. COVID-19 presented an opportunity for us to learn how strong perception can be, and how heavily that can weigh on our sense of well-being.

Truth

Truth lies in the middle. That things can be horrible and wonderful all at the same time; a difficult concept for humans to embrace because we need to categorize things.

We can see the gifts, while recognizing the horror. We can experience joy, while honoring pain. Our experience can matter, while someone else's equally matters. We can create space for all of these things because all are true.

The truth is, COVID-19 brought so much destruction, and so. many. gifts. Gifts of awareness, of growth and opportunity, of time, of space, of connection, gifts of realization, of experience, of being human. We can continue to grow in this truth and we can continue to allow this truth to foster our wellness, our relationships, and our journey, if and when we choose.

About Brittany

My name is Brittany. I'm a licensed therapist, award winning life coach, and intuitive healer. I also am the host of a YouTube show, Get Your Shift Together. As a child and teenager, I struggled with anxiety and panic disorder, depression, substance abuse, low self-esteem, and later on in my life, an abusive relationship. I spent years medicated and in therapy.

For the past 10 years, I've worked as a healer. My journey started as a psychic/medium and Reiki healer where I connected to my clients energy to help them overcome obstacles mentally, emotionally, spiritually and physically. I opened my healing and spiritual development center in 2014 where I went on to win awards as a top ten life coach in Connecticut, top ten best energy healing services, and top ten spiritual development center.

As my practice evolved, so did my business. I obtained a Masters in Science for clinical counseling and my license as a clinical therapist. I specialize in anxiety, depression, women's empowerment, life changes, manifesting, wellness, lifestyle, and trauma. In 2019, I made the decision to move my business to an entirely online based platform for coaching and classes. When I'm not working "as a coach," I enjoy hiking, writing, eating … so much eating … cooking, crafting, and tequila.

Instagram @brittanylunashift

Website: www.britanyluna.com

"Our perceptions are shaped based on our belief systems. What we believe, we will see."

Brittany Luna, M.S.

Connecticut, United States

CHAPTER 18

Fear of Food: How a Global Pandemic Reflects Your Relationship With Food & Your Body

ELIZABETH HALL

What did you first do when you heard that COVID-19 was spreading?

Like most people, when I heard we may need to stay in our houses for a few weeks, I headed to the grocery store. But unlike most people, instead of buying toilet paper, I bought eight pounds of butter.

Eight pounds of butter? Of course! It makes perfect sense. When we are in fear we turn to old habits and patterns that have brought us comfort in the past. Butter had always been one of those sources of comfort to me.

As a kid, I used to melt butter in a little pan on the stove and add brown sugar and eat it straight with a spoon. I told myself I was making chocolate chip cookies, but somehow the cookies never appeared, while the butter and sugar disappeared.

I didn't know it at the time, but I was seeking comfort in that butter and sugar. It was a "hit" of dopamine for me. It offered both pleasure and excitement. There was also an air of danger in doing something that I felt like I probably shouldn't be doing as well as the gratification when the mission was accomplished.

There was also the shame and guilt. Why did I do such a weird thing with my food?

And there I was, 40 years later, not even realizing that I was instinctively seeking comfort by buying butter during a global pandemic.

I was in good company. People all over the world were finding themselves in their homes with lots of time on their hands and feeling uncomfortable about their relationship with food.

Many people expressed fear that they would gain the "quarantine 15" and others worried about how to eat healthily and continue with their fitness routines during the pandemic.

Clearly, when life becomes complex and unpredictable-food becomes an issue.

But what people don't realize is that the food isn't actually the issue.

What we do with food or how we feel about exercise is a symptom of our lack of trust, faith, and understanding about our bodies and about the world.

What we do with food is a symptom of how we process our emotions.

It's a symptom of how our bodies have responded to past traumas and have tried to protect themselves.

It's a symptom of growing up in a culture that judges people based on external appearance and spends little time fostering inner resilience.

It's a symptom of people trying to be perfectionists and please other people with their bodies.

It's a symptom of people trying to be "good" where "good" is currently defined as thin.

It's a symptom of not knowing how to handle our stress.

It's a symptom of the cultural expectations we are all trying to fulfill. In addition to being thin, be rich, be athletic, be smart, be successful.

It's a symptom of the oppression and inequity in our systems and lack of access to jobs, education, and medical care in addition to food.

It's a symptom of systemic racism and bias and stigma towards our colors, our abilities, our genders and our weight.

It's a symptom of the lack of self-compassion and self-love that we can access within ourselves.

It's a symptom of how disconnected to self we are.

It's a symptom of our limiting beliefs concerning how the world works and what is possible.

It's a symptom of our core feeling of "not-enoughness" that we are constantly trying to assuage.

It is NOT about laziness, willpower, sugar addiction, or "trying harder."

Who knew that our relationship with food could be so complicated?

What we do with food is a brilliant effort by our bodies to maintain homeostasis. It's no wonder we turn to food for comfort and as an attempt to feel like there is something we can control in our lives.

Yet, what ends up happening is we add more stress, fear, and judgment about our food on top of the stress, fear, and judgment we may have already been feeling.

When you fear weight gain during a time of stress, it is actually your conditioned and programmed response to turn towards something you think you can control-your food and your weight-to distract you from something you can't control.

Take COVID-19, for example.

Talk about uncertainty. Talk about lack of control. Talk about fearing the unknown.

If there was ever a time to have an issue with food, now would be it.

Focusing on our weight feels way more manageable than focusing on job loss, sickness, and death.

And yet, facing what is hard is the only way through it. This was one of the invitations and the gifts of COVID. The opportunity to stand and face our fears. To go within. To use the power of the pause to tap into our inner guidance and our inner strength and to cultivate resilience.

COVID gave us a chance to turn toward healing and learn how to source our own safety from within because it sure wasn't going to be coming from without.

Healing our relationship with our inner selves is the path to healing our relationship with food. This is an inside job, not an external one. Keto, the Whole 30, and Paleo are not going to bring you the peace and ease that you seek.

Replacing the shingles on the outside of the house is not going to help if the roof is leaking.

Meaning, we could spend our entire lives (and many people do) trying to get our bodies and our accomplishments to match what society says they should look like.

But, if we don't have an internal sense of gratitude, love, and acceptance for ourselves, then it doesn't matter what we achieve, we will always feel like we are not enough.

You are not broken but when did you become so disconnected from your body and your wholeness? When did you start feeling like you weren't enough? What has been the cost of that disconnection?

We've been barking up the wrong tree for a long long time and focusing on behaviors such as dieting, working out, tracking, measuring, restricting, bingeing, eating clean, fasting, and juicing rather than looking at the thoughts, feelings, lived experiences, social inequities, and emotions that are at the root of our behaviors.

We were never taught that bodies are supposed to vary in shape, size, color, and ability and that's what makes us all so beautiful.

None of this was your fault.

Now, it's time for a journey back to trust in our bodies. This journey is not linear and is different for every body because every body has a different story.

However, there are four main components that will help create a future with more ease, joy, and freedom with food and body if you so choose.

These components are: awareness, self-compassion, embodiment, and trust.

Your path to peace begins with awareness since we can't change what we are not aware of. When did these habits begin? What am I afraid of if I stop? What is the worst that I think will happen?

What are the beliefs I have that drive my relationship with my body and food? Are they really true? What am I assuming? What am I ignoring? If this wasn't about food, what would it be about?

This is the beauty of the pause we have had with COVID. Many people have had plenty of time for reflection and introspection. What do you know now that you didn't before?

What do I value? How do my choices align with my values? Am I making my choices out of fear or love? These questions can be asked about our food, and more importantly, they can be asked about everything else that affects our lives.

In addition to awareness, we absolutely must invest in self-compassion. There is nothing wrong with what we are doing. There is no good or bad to judge ourselves by. We are always doing the best we can with what we have in the moment.

Having self-compassion allows our system to calm down and regulate rather than heaping judgment upon judgment on ourselves and adding fuel to the fire or salt to the wound.

Self-compassion, self-compassion, self-compassion. Over and over again.

How can you accept and allow what is here now in the present moment without judgment?

From this space, we have more internal capacity to see more possibilities and to realize that there is always a choice.

There is a choice in what we think, there is a choice in how we feel, and there is a choice in what we do.

Self-compassion also gives us permission to feel whatever we are feeling without censoring or disconnecting. We don't have to please anyone else-this is our journey.

It's all ok.

Self-compassion is the practice of getting out of the mind and dropping into the heart and letting it lead the way. We let go of the stories we have been telling ourselves and allow our intuition to have a voice.

Now we are getting somewhere. A feeling of relief settles in even as I write this.

Next up, embodiment. Now that we have disarmed the system, how can we get more in touch with the body? Do you feel your internal sensations such as hunger and fullness? Do you honor them?

Where in your body do you feel your feelings? How often do you pause and sense what you feel? How often do you make pleasure a priority?

Breathe.

Feel.

Connect.

Learn to follow your instincts. Learn to honor your impulses. Dance, run, rest, scream, laugh, and cry.

Which brings us to trust. We will never learn to trust ourselves if we rely on external rules and conditions and if we make decisions based on fear or what other people think.

When we trust, we realize that the mind is not the one in charge.

We learn to listen to our inner guidance. We open and let love lead the way and we let it be easy. We trust that our bodies know what to do without our micromanaging.

We trust that we will always have what we need and we are always ok. We trust that even when something goes "wrong" it is still working out for our highest good. We trust in a higher power, a power that is fueled by love.

We surrender and detach from outcomes (a certain weight, a specific job, that person you have your eye on) and know that things are working out exactly as they are supposed to.

Going forward, if we apply these principles in our relationship to self, we will find that our relationship with food becomes more peaceful as well.

Recently, I was cleaning out my garage during the COVID purge and contemplating what was going to happen next during this incredible time of awakening. I was also listening to a podcast and I heard an interesting fact.

It turns out that in Germany they have a saying "Alles in butter." Apparently back in the middle ages, they used to pour melted butter over breakables in order to move from place to place. The butter would solidify and protect fragile dishes.

The phrase "Alles in butter" is now used to mean "All is well." So maybe there is a reason I have always been drawn to butter. Maybe in a past life, I was a German in the middle ages?

Buying the butter helped me to be aware of my own fears and my own need for comfort. I was then able to have compassion for myself and those who were struggling all over the world.

To cope I made sure to move my body and connect with nature and pleasure during the quarantine and I practiced connecting to my heart.

I listened to and trusted my body to do what it needed to do. I knew on a soul level that even when things are not going to be easy, it is also still true that all is well.

ABOUT ELIZABETH

Elizabeth Hall is a Certified Professional Life Coach and Intuitive Eating Counselor who specializes in introducing women to more joy and ease in their relationship with food and their bodies using a weight neutral, holistic approach to healing. Her coaching incorporates mind, body, and spiritual elements that assist women in better understanding the emotional and energetic roots of their body dissatisfaction so they can heal from chronic dieting, binge eating, emotional eating, and more. As women learn to trust the innate wisdom of their own bodies, they experience a ripple effect and are able to find more peace and freedom and joy in multiple areas of life. When Elizabeth is not reading a book on the neuroscience of change or weight science or listening to a podcast on binge eating or self-care, she can be found walking her dog, eating a meal with her family, or napping on the porch.

Website: www.elizabethhallcoaching.com

"If we don't have an internal sense of gratitude, love, and acceptance for ourselves, then it doesn't matter what we achieve, we will always feel like we are not enough."

ELIZABETH HALL

Connecticut, United States

CHAPTER 19

How to Trust Your Body and Find Your Truth

CHRISTINE RAPP DOMBROWSKI, PhD

Sometimes our truths lie deep within our heart. We aren't even necessarily aware of them until they suddenly surface when two things happen: something in our life triggers them and we are ready to take that truth and journey with it. Quarantine became an opportunity for all of us to settle in this way, to quiet our lives and open ourselves to allow our truths to surface.

One evening at the beginning of the quarantine, as I was sitting down at the end of the day, I suddenly had the thought, "I trust my body." I instantly responded with the thought, "No, I don't." That immediate reaction was the start of a profound journey of self-discovery, empowerment and self-love throughout the next months. Many questions followed. Why would I have this thought "I trust my body" to begin with? Why would I immediately deny it? How could I not trust my body? Why don't I trust it? What does it even mean to trust my body? How can I move to trust it especially during a time of worldwide pandemic?

It seems so natural to think that we trust our bodies. We all live in our bodies every day. We use them to move in the world. We see them in the mirror and think that is who I am. There is no denying that we are connected to our physical forms and also reliant on them. Yet, I am going to argue that we really aren't raised to trust our bodies or to connect with them and learn their signals and powers. Instead, we are taught to look outside ourselves to define their worth and needs and to separate ourselves from them and mistrust and deny them. It is time to reconnect with our bodies so that we can begin to live fully spiritual lives. This journey, if we wish, dives deep into beliefs about our physical bodies and how we relate to them and then allows us to open ourselves more to our intuitive guidance and to step into our complete power-body, mind and soul.

The only things you need to start connecting more deeply with your body is to approach it with compassion and love. There is no room for judgement here. To be honest, this journey is on-going and will be, I suspect, a journey through lifetimes. So, what I share with you here are just three key new beliefs, which are allowing me to live my life from the core truths of who I am, and which are part of a much larger healing that is taking place on the level of the conscious self, the physical self, and the soul self. Maybe they will speak to you, too.

Key New Belief 1: My body is a wondrous and dynamic system with a wisdom of its own.

Old Belief: I need to strive to maintain a static, unchanging physical form.

Over the past few years, I have been moving more and more to a place where I am trusting and confident in my body. Much of the freeing I needed to do was about beliefs and attitudes I had accepted as truths. They dealt with socio-cultural ideals, family beliefs and attitudes, and truths fed to me by the outside world from birth. In a way, it is difficult to unweave these beliefs from one another. So often they are tightly enmeshed with each other. So, for example, when I believe that I need to maintain my youth to remain relevant, this belief ties in to: my worth, my self-acceptance, my identity, how I relate to others, how I care for my body, how I see myself as a sexual being, how I approach aging, what I define as beautiful, etc.

Society tells me, if I look like I did in my twenties-thin and youthful, then I am beautiful and, therefore, worthy, accepted, and relevant. We see this in media, advertising, throughout the entertainment industry, the fashion and beauty industry, and maybe even from the people in our lives. Men and women alike are shown consistently every day what our ideal of beauty should be, and it is all about youth and, in most cases, maintaining impossibly extreme physiques. In addition, each family adds its own beliefs about beauty, health, and worth. My family believed that to be worthy and respected you needed to be thin. Being thin showed discipline and worth through beauty. It even showed social class and gentility in my parents' eyes. These beliefs run back through generations and generations, through centuries and millennia.

As a young child, I accepted what the world and my parents told me about my body as unquestioned truth. It is these childhood truths, which we take deep into ourselves often at a subconscious level. We hold them without even realizing how deeply they have taken root or how they shift and move within our minds and shape who we believe ourselves to be. As children we don't even question the validity when someone defines for us who we are. Adults tell us we are the smart one, or the nice one, or the sporty, nerdy, difficult one. We take this as our unquestionable truth. Only now am I beginning to break away and question each belief or attitude I hold about my body (there are definitely more that will surface as I go). It begins with moments of realization and awareness, like when I was gifted with the thought, "I trust my body." Becoming aware brings me the gift of perspective and from there the opportunity of choice.

I hadn't realized or even thought about whether I trusted my body. I just had a body. I never thought about having a symbiotic relationship with it. Now that I have this awareness that my body is here for me for a reason, I can choose to keep these childhood and societal beliefs as my truth or I can let them go and replace them with ones, which better serve me. The beautiful thing is once awareness starts, it will keep revealing new layers to your beliefs, allowing you to delve deeper and deeper into re-discovering the true you. It is a process of empowerment and love and wonder, if you allow yourself to open up to it.

Reflection Questions: Do you trust your body to journey through life in all its stages? Do you find yourself trying to manipulate, control, or fit your body into a shape other than the one it has now? If you do, look at the motives behind this wanting to change. Sometimes they come from a desire to live your best life, because you want to be healthy, for example. But don't be afraid to look deeper and see if there are voices other than your own telling you why you need to stop your body's natural changes. Ask yourself, how do these reasons make you feel? Do you feel they come from a loving and compassionate place? Or do they come from fear (fear of aging, fear of illness, fear of irrelevance in the eyes of society, fear of pain ...) Or do the desires to change your body come from a desire to be healthier, to have a body that is able to continue your life doing all the things you love or, maybe, to heal an illness? Taking time to feel into the why you are moved to take any action in life is always a powerful tool to help you live most authentically and to live from truth and love.

Old Belief: My body doesn't have an intelligence, it is just a vessel for me to live this earthly life.

Becoming aware of my body's wisdom was a process of building a mindful connection with it. I was introduced to the idea of just sitting with my body, checking in with it, and really becoming aware of what it was telling me during my first silent retreat. Just sitting with my mind and body wasn't about acknowledging and moving on; it wasn't about ignoring or denying; it wasn't about judging or changing. It was about a simple, open awareness of me. It was worth the time to just check in with my body and ask it how am I doing right now. All I needed to do was listen. I found that once I started to pay attention and to listen, my body didn't have to scream so loudly to get my attention. I began to use my body's signals to recognize how I was doing in any given moment, to situations and thoughts I was having. I began to recognize, for example, when I was feeling good and when I was stressed much sooner than before. I began to communicate with my body. I was becoming connected to it and I was responding to its messages to address imbalances.

I am still working through what this means for me. It's a process after all, not something you can accomplish in one moment. In fact, I feel like it is a life's journey for us to work on this body/mind reconnection. It means seeing how blocked we are to receiving or interpreting our bodies' messages. For me, one example is my migraines. I have had migraines for about six years now. They happened pretty regularly every two weeks or so and lasted three days. My first inclination when they started was just to power my way through to put up with the pain and just keep living the way I had been. When it became impossible for me to continue living with them, I consulted a neurologist, who prescribed several different medications to try. I did try them, one made me so sleepy I couldn't function and the other had no effect at all. So I continued on, changing nothing, looking at nothing about my life that might be causing this. The doctor's answer had been medication and that hadn't worked, so there was nothing more to do for them.

Then in 2016 I had a stroke. There may, or may not, be a connection between my migraines and the stroke. I will never know, but the important thing is the stroke forced me to stop and to slow my life down. I could no longer ignore my body's messages. My body made its message known to me in a way I could not ignore. I needed to stop working at the pace I was working. I needed to pay attention to myself. I need to care and love myself. I needed to look closely at my life and see what was failing or missing and what was working for me. Over the next two or three years, I slowly gained back my energy. My brain slowly woke up again, not the same as before, but in a new more sensitive and mindful way. Some of this was a conscious choice, some of it was required due to my body's stepping in and demanding it.

In the two years of fatigue and rest, I had time to really explore my health via my body. I was able to look at how I was eating. I was able to see what it might be like to take a break and give myself respite when I needed it, to try not to carry heavy expectations for what productive days looked like, to let go of perfectionism, to let go of labels, to begin to care and love myself. This mindful way of approaching your relationship with your body does not need to come from illness, as it did with me, it can be nurtured at any moment you decide to embrace the gift your body is and to trust it.

Our bodies carry a wisdom and we need to begin to access and listen to that wisdom.

Reflection Questions: Do you spend time with your body? Do you consciously slow down and allow yourself moments of quiet to focus on how your body is doing and listening to what it has to tell you? Mindfulness is the key to beginning to connect with your body's wisdom, to begin to understand how it uniquely communicates with you, and then how to work with your body to move towards building emotional and physical wellness and health. Meditation, body scans, intuition, and internal guidance along with patience are some ways to achieve this body-self connection.

Key New Belief 2: My body is one of my greatest gifts given to me in this life.

Old Belief: I need experts to guide me in how to understand and care for my body.

Science tells me that I need to seek advice about my body and its health from medical professionals and to rely on their medication and treatment before even connecting with my own body's wisdom. To add to this, society tells me to ignore illness and pain and instead to be "strong" and to place everything and everyone before my own well-being. Not only are we conditioned to believe that experts solely hold the wisdom about what our bodies are saying and what they need, but we are also told to ignore the signals our bodies send us to let us know something is wrong.

One aspect of this conditioning ties into the idea that to feel emotional or physical pain is weak. We hold beliefs about strength coming from enduring pain and going on despite it. It doesn't teach us to ask ourselves why our bodies even send us pain signals and then what we should do with these signals. Physiological and emotional pain have a function. It is our cue to pay attention. From fostering this awareness or connection with our physical and emotional condition, we can assess how we are doing in that moment and take the opportunity to shift perspectives and make changes to bring us back to optimum well-being. This may entail looking to traditional medical help or holistic help, but always first checking in with ourselves. You just need to be connected with your body and trust its signals to help guide you in achieving your best well-being.

Sometimes our bodies need to send stronger messages when we don't pay attention to the quieter ones. Several years ago, I woke up in the middle of the night and as I opened my eyes, I clearly heard "Everything's going to be ok," and then my world started spinning. That was the night I had my stroke and it changed the trajectory of my life. I am eternally grateful for that experience, although the shift to a new life wasn't always easy. As I stepped more and more into connecting with my body after having a stroke, I began to marvel at it and to respect it as having a wisdom and knowing of its own.

It turns out my body had been speaking to me for several years before the stroke. Speaking to me about how I was not managing my stress; how I was ignoring my intuition; how I was living a life that was separate from who I really was.

Having a stroke forces you to listen. Exhaustion, brain fog and issues with reading, coordination, all forced me to stop and pay attention. I began to learn that though medical doctors and experts have some answers they don't have all of them. Where they can speak of "the average" they cannot speak of the individual. Only I can do that. Only I can speak from knowledge of what my body needs. I realized I needed to be able to speak for and advocate for my body and work with these experts and not give over all my power to them. My body and I are now a team. We communicate. I listen. We work together. We trust each other.

For me, accessing my body's intelligence, learning to understand its language and listening to its messages has been a journey of realizing that my body is a magnificent tool, and I am lucky to have it as my partner. Take a moment to reflect on the magical complexity of the human body. It is a universe unto itself. It is intricate, delicate, and mysterious. Just think of the many physiological functions that still are not completely understood from the brain and the neurological system, to the gut and its own biome which corresponds to every part of your body, to the heart, and its role as the body's second brain. Becoming mindful of the messages your body is constantly sending you frees you from disempowering beliefs that you are at your body's whim and that your body and its functions are separate from the soul. Living an earthly life requires both soul and body, so it seems only logical that there needs to be a complimentary and necessary relationship between the two.

Reflections Questions: Are there aspects of your well-being, whether physical or emotional, where you have been getting messages that all is not as good as it could be? Sometimes these messages come in physical symptoms, like pain or discomfort, sometimes in emotions like anger or frustration, sometimes in recurring thoughts like, "I should look into why I feel this pain," or "I wonder why I always get so frustrated and lash out at Person A," or "I would so love to learn to paint." All of these thoughts are directional. They are guideposts showing you a new direction to shift towards to begin healing and addressing imbalances and illness in your body, your emotional body, and/or your life.

Key New Belief 3: I am enough. My body is enough.

Old Belief: I need to change and alter my body and work towards this consistently to bring about better health, fitness, abilities.

There is this idea we have been given that our bodies are our enemies. We see them as something we need to control. We see ourselves not as our body's partners, but as our body's master. We focus on them only to see the lack, the illness, the pain, and we feel we need to use discipline, focus, and demands to control them. We rarely celebrate them and honor our bodies for all they do for us every second of every day. We can go about all the complexities of daily life and do extraordinary things because of our bodies. We so often work towards maintaining them in one perfect form or wishing them to be other than they are-pain free, thinner, stronger, perfect.

There is often this constant striving for perfection of a given ideal. Perfection of our outward looks, our nutrition, our exercise, our stress levels, our happiness, our pleasures. Yet, in exactly this striving, we do two things. We are living outside of this moment and not enjoying what it brings us, because we are always looking ahead to some goal or ideal rather than embracing and honoring where we are right now. We expect unrealistic things of ourselves and our lives. We need to remember we are here to live a human life, and human life is a whole experience encompassing all possible emotions. Experiencing life allows us to learn and grow, to be inspired and to inspire, to bring our unique perspective to this world. If we live our lives in denial of our complete selves, we cannot achieve what we are meant to achieve.

By accepting where we are in any given moment, by acknowledging what we are feeling and experiencing in our bodies and minds, we honor ourselves and we come to a place where we can move forward into the next moment armed with our body's and mind's wisdom to act in our best interests. Perhaps in times when we are confronted with our fears, our anxieties and our stresses, as in times of COVID-19, we are given an opportunity to turn towards ourselves rather than away. To turn toward these fears, to acknowledge them, to honor how we are feeling, but also to check in with how we are in this moment, not how we project the future to be or to focus outwards to what the world is telling us. Gaining perspective is where our power rests, because when we gain perspective we have the opportunity to choose differently and in choosing we have our power. Trust your body, it is enough in this moment on your life's journey.

Reflections: Do you tend to want to master your body? Do you hold beliefs that your body will turn on you or has turned on you, as in illness or chronic pain? What do you expect from your body? Or do you expect nothing from your body? Do you even think about your body and its needs?

There is a reason we are giving physical bodies to live out our lives. It seems to me we are meant to have an intimate relationship with them. This intimacy only comes when it is nurtured and fostered in our lives. As with any other relationship, we need to spend time with each other, we need to show each other love and respect, compassion and attention. Trust is necessary for those moments when we aren't able to communicate clearly, or don't have time to have a full conversation about something or maybe even can't completely grasp or understand what is going on at all levels. Trust implies that we accept that our bodies only want what is best for us and are helping us attain that. There is a balance needed as well. Our bodies trust us to make the decisions for our highest and best, and we trust our bodies to let us know when things are not functioning well. One needs the other to complete our life's journey as we are meant to do. If we work as partners, we can traverse through our life journey fully in touch with ourselves, for we are, after all, body, mind and spirit. Trust and you will live from a place of your most authentic truth.

About Christine

Christine is an energy healer, spiritual teacher, and author. As a curious student of all things spiritual, she has devoted the past thirty years of her life to the study and practice of spirituality and mysticism. Her passion for teaching and writing focuses on her sharing what she has learned on her own journey of discovery and empowering others to live their own spiritual life based on their own truths. In 2008 she completed her PhD in female Christian mysticism at the University of Pennsylvania. She has studied and uses various healing modalities in her work, including Reiki, Holographic Sound Healing ©, Metatron Colour Healing™, Mindfulness, and Astrology.

Website: www.finding-dharma.com

"Our bodies are our gifts allowing us to take this journey and if we work as partners we can traverse through our lives fully in touch with ourselves for we are, after all, body, mind and spirit."

Dr. Christine Rapp Dombrowski

Connecticut, United States

CHAPTER 20

The Essentials of Self-Care to Survive and Thrive

KRISTI H. SULLIVAN

Have you ever experienced a time when life unexpectedly turned you upside down or knocked you sideways? I'm talking about one of those times or perhaps a year (like 2020!) when you just want to hit "reset?" But before I get to 2020...let me share a bit about my journey and how essential self-care has helped get me through challenging times – to not only survive but thrive.

Right before COVID-19, I had been having an intense two-year period in my life. I had experienced a family crisis, a marriage crisis, and a job crisis – each initially left me feeling knocked down, without the hope of recovery or repair. Each situation brought up difficult and sometimes traumatic emotions, like panic, rage, anger, frustration, despair, grief, and sadness.

In 2018, I got a startling phone call in the middle of the night from my mother in a panic. My father, who had been diagnosed with Alzheimer's years earlier, awakened my mother and dragged her out of bed while frantically yelling "we need to leave, we need to leave" in his native Polish language. The result for him was a visit to the hospital to stabilize his behavior affected by this terrible disease–and for me, all that was happening triggered anxiety, lack of control, and fear.

Later that year, my nearly 20-year marriage began to unravel. While its foundation crumbled with heart-wrenching loss for over a year, my world was rocked by avalanches of hurt, shame and despair. I lost my sense of trust and faced uncertainty about the future of a marriage that I had defined.

Fast forward to early 2020, I was about to celebrate a 20-year anniversary at my job–only to find out shockingly that I was getting eliminated from the company, which was like family to me since day one. I felt like the floor suddenly went out from under me, after holding on to an identity for far too long-leaving me feeling anger, disappointment, and grief.

And then COVID-19 happened in 2020, a year that turned everyone's world upside down, sideways, or twisted completely.

Why is COVID-19 happening for us?

We're in a great period of uncertainty. As I write this chapter, we are not sure when the end of COVID-19 is in sight. Some feel that the virus has forced us to be in isolation, disrupted our routines, and created overwhelm. While all of this is true, I have realized I have the opportunity to slow down, to practice being in solitude, and to turn inward to learn the effects of this global situation and understand what I need to get through this unfamiliar crisis.

During times of crises, our emotions can be all over the place, and often can be negative and in a place of fear and worry. Uncertainty is not comfortable–and we are creatures that tend to prefer comfort. As I have come to learn, the opportunity for growth usually comes during our time of discomfort and uncertainty. As we experience hardships and challenges, it can often lead to our greatest lessons in life and opportunities for personal growth and evolvement–to survive and thrive.

What opportunities has COVID-19 given us?

We're in a great period of change. Systems have been disrupted, and habits have been upset–perhaps some of which were unhealthy to us individually or collectively to begin with. I believe that

COVID-19 has provided us with the opportunity to take pause and hit reset. This is a time to evaluate or reevaluate what you need for complete self-care on a daily basis.

During my most challenging times, I have learned that my self-care is my saving grace to not only survive but thrive. I define my self-care as my daily ritual to nurture my body, mind, and spirit. Fortunately, I have had a long-time interest in holistic health and yoga, which began 20 years ago. I learned about the mind-body-spirit connection through yoga, and eventually, I explored and practiced various holistic modalities to heal wounds, self-limiting beliefs and traumas. The self-care practices I have established and continue to create help me get through these life altering events. It's why I'm now on a mission to motivate and educate others to make self-care a daily ritual.

What can we create from the COVID-19 experience for our future?

Let's pause and reset... and focus on self-care now more than ever. We need to heal and evolve, to survive and to thrive.

I believe there are three levels of self-care to help you heal, reprogram and evolve your mind, body and spirit. These three levels of self-care are:

1. Occasional self-care - periodic, time-bound or sporadic activity
2. Daily self-care - commitment to everyday activities
3. Spiritual self-care - deeper, long-lasting actions to evolve and heal

Level 1 - Occasional self-care means you may sporadically exercise, sometimes have periods of eating well, and once in a while take time to slow down (like a vacation). The payoff is short and effects are rarely long lasting. Most individuals may start a self-care routine with the occasional practice. This category includes New

Year's resolutions that are usually cast by the wayside after a few weeks.

Level 2 - Daily self-care means you are committed to following a more regular, consistent schedule–like moving your body in some way for 30 minutes a day, or choosing vegetables and fruits as your daily main food groups. And perhaps going to bed each day at a reasonable time to get enough sleep, to rejuvenate and feel rested every morning. While individuals at this level may sometimes have the occasional slip (a late night, or sweet treat, or a day skipping exercise), they go right back to a daily routine because they are (key word) "committed" and have created recurring habits.

Level 2 sounds ideal and is sometimes the level we aim for achieving–where we set our goal and consider it accomplished if we are committed. BUT I'm challenging you today to set the bar higher because the pay-off is much bigger, longer lasting, and life changing!

Level 3 - Spiritual practice means you are connected to a higher power or your inner wisdom, or ultimately aligned in mind-body-spirit and self-love. In addition to your daily mind-body activity, you also explore what's on the inside. Perhaps it's through journaling, keeping a daily gratitude diary, or praying. Or it's working with a practitioner to address limiting beliefs or old wounds from trauma (which we all have, by the way). It's slowing down, and turning attention from the outside inward to explore how you can evolve even deeper and more fully to expand not only self-love for yourself but to become a light to others. Level 3 is BIG.

It may seem like a lofty aspiration, a dream to become enlightened. But friends, we are all spiritual beings having a human experience–and what does life mean if not a journey for us to evolve fully mind, body and spirit? I urge you to consider which level are you at and if it is really serving you to your fullest potential. Are you at level 1, occasional or sporadic? Or level 2, committed daily? Or can you reach for level 3–a deeper, spiritual practice?

What do your current self-care rituals look like?And I don't mean drinking a glass of wine each night to unwind — or scrolling through Facebook to take your mind off stress... distractions that we can easily turn to (even me, especially in 2020). The self-care I'm talking about serves you in a healthy way. Like consuming nourishing foods to give you energy, and drinking enough water. Like spending time with people who inspire you and enrich your life. Like being kind to yourself and setting boundaries.

I have survived serious times of crisis (COVID-19 included) because I commit to self-care on a daily basis. I also know the importance of support to make this happen. So I recently created a virtual community to motivate and educate women to give themselves permission to make essential self-care a priority. I connect them to the resources and tools to curate daily self-care rituals.

Self-care can help you to pause and reset. It can help you to heal, reprogram and evolve–to expand your mind, body and spirit–to survive and thrive. We all need ourselves and each other to be the light, more than ever.

ABOUT KRISTI

Kristi H. Sullivan is a wellness advocate and self-care expert with a passion for health, wealth and happiness–and helping women thrive. She began her journey nearly two decades ago as a yoga teacher (RYT200) and entrepreneur while culling her communication skills in nonprofit environments. During COVID, Kristi took her business online and now hosts a virtual membership community to connect busy women to resources and support for curating daily self-care rituals. She is a co-author of *The Ultimate Guide to Self-Healing, Volume 2.* In addition to hosting wellness workshops and webinars, she teaches Human Design and the art of aligning with your true self for manifesting abundance.

Facebook @Kristi's Self Care Tribe.

Website: www.kristisselfcare.com

"Self-care can help you to pause and reset. It can help you to heal, reprogram and evolve–to expand your mind, body and spirit–to survive and thrive. We all need ourselves and each other to be the light, more than ever."

KRISTI H. SULLIVAN

Connecticut, United States

Arise

tsunamis

phoenix

surrender

truth

embrace

CHAPTER 21

Roaring Us Awake

KARLA ARCHAMBEAULT

I've always had dreams of tsunamis, the kind that sweep in out of nowhere, taking everything, chasing me, hunting me. I'm always running, hiding, trembling in my heart, feeling into the void-like chasm of impending doom. I usually escape successfully.

This time it caught me, overcame me, took me, and shook me to my core. It said, 'Stop WASTING your TIME! Stop wasting your energy on things that don't fulfill you anymore!' Or as Dr. Clarissa Pinkola Estes wrote so poignantly and painfully in *Women Who Run With the Wolves*, 'Stop suckling a dead litter!'

Just stop. A forced, blessed stop, a benevolent genie of 'stop,' granting my secret wish for something that puts an end to all that I am not brave enough to end on my own. It's been ingeniously disguised as a virus. Pausing what has been and surrendering to the tsunami of the unknown felt utterly terrifying. It can feel powerful, dark, and sometimes violent as it tears through our lives and our realities, shaking, and roaring us AWAKE.

COVID-19 woke me up to see what I'm holding onto, and what's no longer working. What is past its expiration date. In my life, and in the world. When news of the virus hit, I had been doing bodywork and energy healing at Kripalu for almost ten years, but in my spirit knew that I needed to be shifting my energies to creating my own business and working towards that. The honest truth is that I had been getting bored with spa work, the back-to back-clients, and no continuous connection or getting to develop any real depth in relationship to my clients. My body and spirit were starting to hurt. I needed a break and to make some real changes.

One thing to know about me is that I live alone. Well, I live with my cat, so that's not really fair to say. But this stop time and social isolation became a forced meditation retreat. Just me and my own energy, my own thoughts, my own terror, and anxiety. No touching anyone, or doing any of my hands-on healing work. I needed to pull all of my energy in and to call my spirit back to me. Just me.

It might sound weird, but I've always had fantasies of stopping time. I want to stop time because the relentless march of time can feel so dizzying and unsatisfying. Like all of the back-to-back bodywork sessions, life can seem to move at a breakneck speed, with no time to breathe and appreciate. I've wanted to pause the movie, so I can say to the people I love, 'I love you, I'm honored to know you, thank you for walking this path with me.' I really mean it. The level of gratitude I frequently feel for this life and for all of my friendships and soulmates that are here with me is just HUGE. So often, things move so fast that we don't often get to pause in sacred space, eye to eye, heart to heart, with those that we love. This time has brought me into a much deeper gratitude for all the little things, for my friendships and to a greater sense of my purpose as a healer, here on earth.

COVID-19 has also given me the gift of seeing what I want to keep. Through this time I have come to know deeply that I love touching people. I love doing my healing work, I love to help connect people deeply to their bodies and their feelings, to provide them with a nourishing space to heal and feel. It gives me a sense of true purpose. I love everything about healing and transformation and embodiment. I love our senses. I love connecting in groups, dancing, playing, laughing, eating, and relaxing. It is who we are. I miss that so much.

What did I witness? What blessings did COVID-19 bring?

Everyone was so scared it seemed. But as I tuned into the deeper messages amidst the fear and chaos, I could also feel this benevolent force behind this tsunami which was challenging to speak about. This benevolent force was sweeping through the collective heart of humanity, connecting us all to the heart of the matter, the root cause of our suffering and disconnection. The collective insanity of a world going at warp-speed and starving for a deeper and more meaningful existence. I felt profoundly that sometimes what we think we want, and what we actually need to grow our souls, are two very different things.

I witnessed humanity come together which is no small thing. People we hadn't seen or spoken to reached out to us, or us to them, like an invisible bridge of love became visible all of a sudden. Connecting us like the interconnected roots of old growth trees. WE are truly one being, which breathes together, inhale, and exhale. I felt a softening in my heart around long held anger and pain. A forgiveness came in...a lowering of the sword and shield around my heart.

I now see just how interconnected we all are. And with this insight comes the responsibility for each of us to change what's no longer working. To set our minds and hearts towards the creation of the new world we want to see be born.

Upon reflection, I truly stand in awe of what a powerful time we are in, as we hang in the balance between the old and the new. Humanity is now like a woman in labor, deep in the throes of an ancient life giving process. Push, push, birth! She stands between the two worlds, and we are midwifing the future.

I ask us to ask ourselves these questions, and hold a prayer to spirit in my heart for their timely answering.

Can I/you/we allow the elements of nature to purify us and the tsunamis to sweep through our houses, our souls, our world?

Can I/you/we surrender?

Can we open to a new, more glorious energy? True. Raw. Real.

Will we be the medicine? Individually? Collectively?

Can I/you/we trust the steady drumbeat of our hearts? The earth's heart?

Can I steady myself to hear and feel and see clearly, that I might follow my truth, my heart, my destiny?

I believe the heartbeat of the earth is calling us to joy.

Calling us to sun-drenched lands. Soul-soaked vistas.

Let the powerful elements of the earth and of your very body guide you.

Plant your heart seeds; water your soul.

Guard your precious soul-seedlings; ignite your passions.

Cut decisively what no longer serves.

Nourish, feed, be a home for the hearts of all beings.

May you pull up the weeds of injustice and hatred in your own heart.

May you not fear the darkness within, and know that it is the raw material for your very LIFE FORCE, your POWER, your BEAUTY, and your POTENCY.

May you be bathed by the light of the sun and illumination of the stars.

May you be filled with delight, joy, and divine purpose.

Sometimes we get everything we've prayed for and more.

You are the medicine. You are the Light.

Do not forget this precious moment in time.

Allow this time to change you, grow you, to heal your heart.

Let the tsunami tear through your heart. Let it get you, let it change you.

Let it cleanse and clear you and awaken your heart to new and more wildly magical possibilities.

Let it open you to the greatest mystery of all:

Your wild, precious, vulnerable and beautiful human life.

Bless the storms, and bless the gentle rains.

May they clear and cleanse and awaken our hearts.

About Karla

Karla Archambeault LMT, RSMT is an inspirational and visionary holistic health practitioner who is dedicated to healing and integrating the psyche and soma of humanity.

Karla maintains Adhara Sacred Wellness, a heart-centered holistic bodywork and somatic psychotherapy practice in the Berkshires. Karla has spent the past decade working at Kripalu Center for Yoga and Health as an Ayurvedic Health Counselor and as a bodywork and energy healing practitioner. She is pursuing her Master's degree in Acupuncture and Chinese Herbal Medicine.

When not working or studying, she enjoys walking in the woods, sitting by the water, getting lost in used bookstores, photography, cooking, dancing, writing, spending time with her sweet black cat, Brahmi, and exploring this beautiful, magical, and wildly precious life.

Website: www.adharasacredwellness.com

"I now see just how interconnected we all are. And with this insight comes the responsibility for each of us to change what's no longer working. To set our minds and hearts towards the creation of the new world we want to see be born."

KARLA ARCHAMBEAULT

Massachusetts, United States

CHAPTER 22

Rising from the Ashes

RYAN D. HALL

"In order for a phoenix to rise from its own ashes,
a phoenix must burn."
–Octavia Butler–

I had massive hopes for 2020. This year was going to see me creating the romantic relationship of my dreams, building an increasingly healthy bank account, building the life coaching business I've been talking about ever since I joined my training program, and publishing the novel manuscript I've been trying to publish for two years. 2020 was going to be the year I created my life on my terms.

As the ball dropped on 2020, I was working my dream job, meeting incredible people, and slowly but surely, I was finding happiness.

But on an unseasonably warm Friday afternoon in early January, I found myself on a park bench in White Plains, New York checking the train schedules for a train for me to leap in front of. One's mind jumps to darkness when one gets fired from one's dream job after having that job for a month.

I'm sitting on that park bench. And I kept having these feelings and thoughts floating inside my mind. Black thoughts. Thoughts like "do I even need to be here anymore?" And feelings of despair I'd never before felt.

After a call to the suicide hotline (yeah, it got that bad) I walked to the White Plains train station. But instead of stepping in front of the 3:15 train to Grand Central, I got ON the 3:15 to Grand Central.

Once I got to New York City, with a feeling like my feet were in quicksand, I started to wander. Wherever my feet carried me, my body followed.

This was January 3rd, 2020. The Saks Fifth Avenue holiday display as well as the 30 Rock Christmas Tree were still up and going. This was well before the phrase "social distancing" became part of the vernacular, so crowds were thick and packed like Gotham Sardines.

Right across the street from Rockefeller Center is St. Patrick's Cathedral. While I'm not Catholic, and I'm not entirely sure I'm Christian, I found myself drawn to her doors, which were wide open.

I walk in and take a deep breath. This is the same building and the same sanctuary that I've seen on TV and in movies countless times. I didn't stay long, but while I was there, I felt something incredibly powerful. A feeling of peace, of wholeness, and of "I Am."

Little did I know how often I'd have to remind myself of this moment as 2020 unfolded.

In many ways, the prologue to my 2020 was how my 2019 unfolded.

My business was tanking. I was working two menial jobs, neither of which kept me afloat. I'd fallen behind in rent and utilities. My landlords threatened me with eviction. And to top things off, my sister back in Alabama was diagnosed with stage III throat cancer.

This is the time in our program when reporters ask Mary Todd Lincoln if she enjoyed her date night with Abraham at Ford's Theatre.

On May 10, 2019, I handed my key back to my former landlords after I'd gotten evicted. After I handed my key back to my now former landlord, I stood on their porch and got cursed out for 30 minutes. At that moment, for all intents and purposes, I was homeless.

Eventually, my dog Pete and I found a pretty good situation. We landed at an Air B and D (the D standing for Dinner) in Stamford, CT, maybe a 20-minute drive from my now former home. As part of my rent, they served dinner almost every night. As we settled in and got comfortable, I realized that my depression wasn't getting any better.

It was a good situation. Good room, some unique roommates–including one who actually knew of my former town in Southeast Alabama because that's where he was originally from, and some really killer food. My roommate Mike is a terrific cook. But I never trusted my landlord there. (Side note: I sure know how to pick out a landlord, y'all.) Truthfully, I was always a little scared of him. A big, burly guy, he could talk an Eskimo into buying ice.

I eventually found full-time employment after a few months and started to feel into myself again. Brought me back to being me a little bit.

Right before the holidays in 2020, I was mindlessly scrolling Facebook when I found what I thought was my dream job. This was a job working as a copywriter for a small advertising agency in White Plains, NY.

When I uprooted my life in Alabama in 2017, I made three promises to myself. Put my heart and soul into my coaching business, publish my second novel, and get into the New York advertising scene as a copywriter.

Within 20 minutes of submitting my application, I received an email looking to schedule an interview. I crushed that interview into a fine powder! The CEO of the company interviewed me herself! I stayed in her office for over an hour!

I was in, y'all! I was in! I got the job and started in early December.

Let's flash forward about a month.

One early February night at dinner, my landlord started in with some bonkers conspiracy theories about what he was seeing coming from overseas. This was well before COVID hit our shores.

I laughed it off as the rantings of an insomniac. At this time, China was building temporary hospitals in a matter of weeks in the Wuhan area. My landlord was also going in with some really weird Bill Gates conspiracy theory. Disturbing to say the least.

I made a joke to him about "what size tinfoil hat are you wearing?" The look he returned to me said "just watch" without saying a word.

All throughout February, he kept making some massive runs to Costco. Tons and tons of food and cleaning supplies. He sent someone to the Best Buy where I was selling vacuums to see about buying a chest freezer. Those had long-since been sold out.

He had a former roommate of mine construct a chicken coop in the backyard. I'm serious, a chicken coop! This would be an easy place for me to make a "flew the coop" joke, but I'll resist.

I simply thought he was making wiser choices about how to keep the house stocked with food and supplies.

I've never been more wrong about anything in my life!

As February wore on, I also managed to pick up a nagging cough that would not go away. I've had bronchitis enough times to know what that felt like, and this felt like bronchitis. I chalked it up to a seasonal illness that visits me...you know...seasonally.

I also didn't have health insurance at the time and with my financial situation as dire as it was, visiting a doctor was out of the question.

The later we got in February, I started getting cryptic text messages from my landlord. "Are you going to be able to catch up on rent? If not, perhaps it's time for you and Pete to make other arrangements."

Full transparency, I did owe a little bit of money. Not a terribly large amount, but I did owe. Working only 16 hours a week, I was hurting really bad trying to keep up with my weekly payments anyway. After my weekly payment, most weeks I might have $30 to last me an entire week.

One Wednesday morning early in March, I was still in bed when my phone chimes with one of those cryptic text messages.

I was out. I was given $1100 cash and was given until noon to pack up and leave. My dog and I were out! He forgave the back money that I owed him.

Looking back on things, he wanted us gone. It wasn't about my dog and me and what I owed him. He was about to clear the house. And while I don't believe I ever had a fever, my cough was getting worse. And with the anxiety and fear going through the world in the early stages of this pandemic, he wasn't taking any chances.

Though he never said this was a reason he kicked me out...I'm not saying it wasn't a reason.

Understand he never spoke to me face to face or even on the phone about this, only by text message.

Just throwing that out there...

I found an inexpensive hotel where Pete and I have been staying ever since, and we're now in June as I write this.

In the early days of this pandemic, I worked hard to avoid the news. If ignorance is bliss, why was I so miserable? I also didn't realize how bad it was getting.

One day in the middle of March, all pro and college sports, concert tours, and theatre shows were postponed. I'll never forget this day–March 12, 2020...my 43rd birthday!

A few weeks after I'd been at the hotel, I ran into one of my old roommates. He was the primary cook in my old place. Mike and I became friends and he told me he picked up whatever had been ailing me and had been coughing like mad. To dump in some lemon juice to the open wound, Mike has an 11-year old daughter who lives part-time with him. It wasn't just me and my dog that he kicked out. It was Mike as well!

It turns out that my landlord kicked everybody out, save for his elderly uncle (who probably would love to leave if he could). He shut everything down. He put the house on lockdown. He even gave me a hard time about my mail that had still been coming to that address!

The biggest lesson I have taken away from the COVID-19 pandemic started with a woman named Ann Ivey Hall. I usually called her Mom. We lost Mom in 2009 after a long illness. Like her Mom before her, she passed away at only 59. Mom was intellectually brilliant and had enough emotional baggage to drive the handlers at LaGuardia to go on strike.

The lesson I'm taking away from this pandemic is one she showed me time and time again.

In one of Mom's more sober moments in her later years, she reflected something to me that I'll take to my grave.

A couple years before she passed, I'd gone after another promotion at a former job. I was an associate for a call center contracted with a major wireless provider. I'd rather not say the name, but think, "Can you hear me now?"

I didn't get the promotion...again. I was tired of being on the phones, and I wanted to show some leadership. In my five years of working for this company, I believe I went after seven promotions, I got turned down for five, and the two promotions I got I didn't really want.

The day I was turned down for promotion number four, I paid my parents a visit instead of making my usual post-work trip to the gym. I was down. I was depressed. And quite frankly, I was angry.

I started talking to Mom about this and she said this to me:

"Ryan, you're the most resilient person I've ever known. You'll be back."

Let's take a look at where I stood when the pandemic started to escalate in early March. I was still working my 16 hours a week job, I was living in a hotel, and my depression was steadily getting worse.

If I could get away with it, I'd stay in the bathtub all day. I'm not exaggerating. I had no motivation, but I also kept going.

It's like a life coaching mentor once said to me, "You love suffering, don't you?"

I suffered. But...I never quit.

I found an ad for a job. This was a company I worked for previously but in a different program. I would be working as a third party vendor for a pretty large company, selling their products inside Best Buy. I'd rather not name the company, but the name rhymes with "bloogle."

I applied.

I performed very well during a virtual job interview.

And I got the job...after waiting out a 2-week hiring freeze.

When you're able to score a full-time job during the middle of a global pandemic, that's nothing to sneeze at.

Four years ago, I made a commitment to myself that I would start a private practice as a life and relationship coach. I spent a lot of money on a training and certification program (worth every dime). I love supporting people to create big, powerful lives and to live the lives of Kings– heart-centered leaders in their world.

My business has, well, it's been tanking. And I'd all but given up on seeing any return on my investment, my time, and my training.

I started working on myself. I started growing myself. I started taking my therapy seriously. I started healing some deep and painful wounds. And I started to see a slow and steady movement and shift in the areas I'm committed to.

And what do you know? With this work, I'm starting to see some growth in my business. Slow, but steady. It's not sustainable yet, but this is a tortoise and hare situation here.

My resilience has always been there. However, I believe this pandemic has shown me what I'm capable of in a really powerful and beautiful way.

The following story may sound like a fictional metaphor, but every word of this story is true.

My grandfather who passed away in 1992 is still one of my greatest heroes. A veteran of the South Pacific, he was awarded the Purple Heart after taking a bullet in the left bicep during the battle of Guadalcanal. When Melborn Ivey returned from his Army deployment, he married his childhood sweetheart and had three kids–the oldest of whom was my mother. He became highly successful in agriculture and real estate with only a fifth grade education. He was also the finest campfire storyteller I ever knew and the biggest reason why I'm a writer today.

I'd love to tell you about *Monkeytown* one day.

Granddaddy had a large farm in rural Houston County, Alabama. And the summer when I was five, my family and I were visiting. We spent most of the summer down there that year since my Grandmother Martha passed away from a massive stroke that May.

On his farm, Granddaddy owned a large herd of cattle. And he also owned a couple of quarter horses that he used to help work his land and his cattle.

Being the typical hard-headed kindergarten graduate I was, I desperately wanted to ride one of those horses by myself. I rode several times with Granddaddy holding me, but I wanted to ride by myself. Granddaddy saddled up Frosty–a filly named so because of a white blaze across her face–and put me up on her. He adjusted the stirrups to fit my short legs and put the rein in my hands.

As Frosty backed out of the stable, I lost my balance and fell on my face. I wasn't injured except for a small cut under my lower lip that a band-aid and some first aid ointment of some kind took care of. This cut left a tiny scar that many years later is still visible in the right light and state of facial hair.

After I fell off Frosty, Mom came sprinting out of the house to check on me. My memory of this event was that I wasn't even crying. I wasn't even hurting. My spirit was in shock.

I wanted to get back up! Mom put her foot down, but I wanted to get back up. I don't remember ever getting to ride Frosty again.

In closing, I don't know if I've learned resilience from the COVID pandemic. But I believe the pandemic has shown me how resilient I already am.

I'd like to leave you with the brilliant words from the chorus of *Laugh About It*, a song by the amazing Tedeschi Trucks Band.

"Rise up, right where they put you down.

Don't let nobody ever, turn you 'round.

Try, try to believe it,

All the caring and hard work and trouble,

Is worth to change."

Humanity is at a low ebb right now. Fear, anxiety, and worry are ruling our consciousness.

If we take a moment, press the pause button, and remember how resilient we all are, this pandemic could be humanity's phoenix rising moment.

Flap those wings.

Create some energy.

Rise up from the embers and ashes and soar!

Soar like never before!

Soar with the eagles.

Rise like the phoenix!

About Ryan

Ryan D. Hall is an author, podcaster, and the life coach for Kings.

As a coach, he's committed to supporting men to get into their hearts and be Kings - the heart-centered leaders of the world.

As a storyteller and podcaster, he's committed to sharing stories of power, redemption, resilience, and heart.

Website: www.royalheartscoaching.com

Podcast: Soul-R-Powered

"If we take a moment, press the pause button, and remember how resilient we all are, this pandemic could be humanity's phoenix rising moment."

RYAN D. HALL

Connecticut, United States

Chapter 23

A Total Surrender to God

Melissa Molinero

Through all this chaos, I have walked with the Lord. It might sound metaphorical, but in the wake of the COVID-19 pandemic, my walk with the Lord has become life itself. I have witnessed firsthand and from many others that in times of great turmoil, we fight to hold onto something or someone that will give us the courage, order, deep understanding, and normalcy we crave. I chose to cling to my creator more than I ever have, and my love and affection for my Heavenly Father has increased.

Have you ever heard the phrase, "What you focus on increases?" In the struggle, the pain, the uncertainty, doubt, fear and unknown, I chose to focus on the only thing that has ever given me the strength and power to create change. Even on my worst days, when I could barely climb out of bed, God's still voice whispered, "Have I not commanded you? Be strong and courageous. Do not be frightened, and do not be dismayed, for the Lord Your God is with you wherever you go" (Joshua 1:9 ESV). When I finally fully accepted that the Lord would not leave me, and allowed Him to take the reins, I realized choosing this power for myself, right there and then, would begin the change in me that would create the change for others.

The pinnacle of this realization for me was when I literally got on my knees, called out to the Lord and asked him, "Lord, show me what you want me to do. Speak to me and tell me how I can make the difference. How can I allow my light to shine on this Earth right now with so much pain and helplessness surrounding us?"

And, as natural as the day begins and ends, I found myself sharing my voice with the world through scriptures, hymns, and songs that have encouraged me in my hardest and darkest moments in life, some of which include the struggles of life during the pandemic.

I cannot say that I was directly affected by the virus itself or that any of my close family members were affected, but seeing the lives lost, the fear and hopelessness of the first responders and medical personnel, and just dealing with a new way of life has been emotionally, physically, and spiritually draining. The thing is, as a leader in the world, I wanted to do something. I wanted to help someone, make a difference for somebody, do anything but sit in my house, isolated from the rest of the world, and closed off in quarantine. We were all experiencing the same thing, yet, in incredibly unique and different ways.

People dying alone, families grieving, close family members and friends clinging to life after spending endless days in a hospital bed, those so afraid to go out and talk to anyone that the thought of going out caused them panic, and those who had taken their own lives out of sheer depression. Screening social media was like putting myself on a roller coaster of emotions in 10 to 15-minute timeframes at a clip and turning on the television was torture to hear the death toll rising and wondering if this would ever end.

Then there are the financial struggles, people losing their jobs thousands at a time, everything closing down, schools being canceled for the rest of the year, parents like myself having to deal with not only our own emotions emerging from this, but how to make our children understand. Trying to see it from the point of view of a six and 12-year-old who cannot fully understand. Going through bouts of tantrums and screaming matches to get them to participate in online schooling, while holding down the household, working from home full-time and trying our best to care for ourselves so we can keep caring for everyone and everything else.

For the first few weeks I remember crying endlessly and praying and praying and praying that things would change, go back to "normal," just be okay. At first, I tried hiding the tears and dealing with it on my own, which only amplified the loneliness I think we all felt. I finally decided to let myself be in process, to be okay with not being okay, and to surrender it all to God. That was when my healing began, and my purpose in this trial was revealed to me. I kept reading and remembering Jeremiah 29:11 (NIV) that states, "For I know the plans I have for you," declares the Lord, "plans to prosper you and not to harm you, plans to give you hope and a future."

I just knew that even at my lowest point, God had a plan for me in this, and more importantly, He has a master plan in this pandemic. Then, something changed in me; something changed because I changed. I started to look at the world's problems with the pandemic as huge possibilities for the plan that God has in all of it. With that major shift in my perspective, I was able to see and create some amazing things.

The Lord has blessed me with so many gifts, talents and interests, and I was able to throw myself into the things I love most to calm my soul, which little by little I realized also soothed the hearts, minds, and souls of so many others who were dealing with the same pain and helplessness I was feeling. Day by day I allowed the Lord's scriptures and songs to flow forth from me and into the public, unworried about how it sounded or what it looked like because I knew if the Lord's mighty love and power could transform me as much as it had in the last few weeks, it could create the same world of change for others.

One of the events I hold so dear to my heart that allowed me to share in God's love and promises is a live video series I was a part of with a ministry I co-lead for my church. We were able to have a Certified Financial Planner come to a live meeting and share her expertise in financial planning during the pandemic, and after the event, we closed with a song I prepared to sing, "I Am Not Alone," by Kari Jobe, which we dedicated to the medical staffs, essential, and frontline workers who so needed to hear that at that very moment, they were not alone in this world.

Once I began to allow the Lord's words to flow forth and become a part of my everyday speech in posts, live videos, here in this book collaboration, and during Bible studies and prayer meetings, my heart filled with joy; waking up in the morning got easier, dealing with the struggle of life in all its change seemed possible, and my fear subsided. And, I saw the change showing up everywhere!

The Lord was and is creating a movement. Now more than ever, in the middle of the pandemic, I see people coming back to the Lord, calling out for protection, and looking to our Creator for the answers. Sometimes when we think the world is falling apart; like we are falling apart, it is the old breaking down to make way for the new; a total breakdown of whatever we have built, thinking we can do it on our own, so, we can humble ourselves and realize that we need God to do that, and that He is the only being that can affect that sort of change within us, and into the world.

Right now, I do not see broken. In all of this, what I see is the glorious works of the Lord taking place in the lives of people everywhere, and I am excited to see how this unfolds. It is truly a wonderful time to be alive! And, we can have the assurance that even in the wake of disaster, we have a God who will never fail us! "He heals the brokenhearted and binds up their wounds" (Psalm 147:3 NIV). Even when we think we have reached our end and there is no more we can give, if we cry out to the Lord, He will bind up our wounds and carry us the rest of the way. For these reasons, I think COVID-19 is happening to us and for us, and the spiritual opportunities it has brought into our lives are massive and unequivocal.

It has been such a beautiful experience to see how God is moving in the lives of everyone right now, and the response in clinging to faith and hope has been critical to say the least. It seems that when pushed to the brink of chaos, people everywhere are calling out to the Lord and looking for something to hold onto. Personally, my faith-walk and relationship with God has grown immensely since COVID-19, and I see a returning back to God, our creator, and the maker of our Universe. I have seen people helping each other, loving their neighbors, and extending a hand to do God's work even when they are feeling in despair. Now, that is not to say that bad things won't occur or haven't occurred and that every person is as kind and generous, but the Lord never promised we wouldn't have suffering, He has promised, however, that He will "never leave us nor forsake us." (Deuteronomy 31:6 NIV).

The transformation I see taking place in the world is just the beginning of larger waves developing, and there are miracles taking shape every second! The word says, "When you are in distress and all these things have happened to you, then in later days you will return to the Lord your God and obey His voice." (Deuteronomy 4:30 ESV). So many of us, including myself, maybe without even realizing it, are hearing and experiencing the voice of the Lord, and what an amazing and awe inspiring journey of opportunities can unfold if we learn to be still and wait on the Lord. (Psalm 46:10 NIV).

Right now we might only see the pain and process that exists in this place, and, maybe this is exactly what needs to happen before we can appreciate what it looks like on the other side. I believe the Lord is preparing our hearts for a level of love and difference that we have never experienced. I want to be here to see it, and I want to share it with all of you. So, maybe instead of dwelling on the worry, the uncertainty, the uncontrollable, the not knowing, and the despair, try shifting your energy to the possibility that exists inside the storm, and what you can create in the darkness.

Making this shift directly rooted in my faith in the Lord has allowed me to see endless opportunities emerging from these waves of change. I see stronger relationships with God, virtual church services allowing God's message to reach the eyes and ears of people on a much grander scale, new leaders in faith rising up to have their voices heard, children following in their parents' footsteps and learning to love and accept their neighbors, brothers and sisters more than ever, deeper and more loving connections and conversations between people, a love and appreciation for God's beautiful Earth and all of its wonders, a greater appreciation for time, prayer, meditation and a unfathomable understanding of faith, God's word, and what it means to exist as part of something bigger in this world. "The greatest rewards come when you give of yourself. It's about bettering the lives of others, being part of something bigger than yourself, and making a positive difference" (Nick Vujicic).

We are all connected, and I think we have lost touch with that. COVID-19 has given us the opportunity to take that back. With the love of God we can push forward, be of service, and think of ourselves as one body; one circle of humanity connected together to do God's work on Earth now! "So, in Christ we, though many, form one body, and each member belongs to all the others." (Romans 12:5 NIV). Everyone in the world is experiencing the same thing at the same time. The power that comes from that deep-rooted connection is remarkable. The best part of it is that we get the opportunity to love each other immensely because that is all we have. To give praise and honor to the Lord for all He has done and all He has blessed us with.

What I dare to dream for our future is a world made entirely from love; a total move in the opposite direction of where we have found ourselves in the past allowing God to be at the epicenter of it. I see a complete revival happening! I see people giving their hearts to the Lord and reclaiming all that God has for them in their lives and the lives of others. I truly see the world in God's hands, and, it all starts with each of us, right here and right now. I see the present circumstance as a tangible choice in how humans want this thing called life to go from here. Sometimes, we have to be completely broken down in order to be built up into something more beautiful.

I see that kind of beauty; the kind that rises from the ashes and has a deep and meaningful direction toward transformation on levels unimaginable.

About Melissa

First and foremost, I am a strong Christian woman with unwavering faith in God. I am also a mom to two beautiful little humans that mean the world to me, a wife of 13 years (and counting!) to the most supportive and loving husband ever, and an ordained Deacon in leadership at Woodcliff Community Reformed Church in North Bergen, New Jersey. I am a Life and Career Coach and Certified Job Counselor in the State of New Jersey offering individual and group coaching sessions, workshops and professional resume writing services to clients everywhere. When I'm not working, spending time with my family, or loving on our two giant Rottweiler fur babies, I enjoy singing and leading worship services at church, reading, writing, spending nights with my girls, lending a hand in my community, stealing getaways to enjoy quiet time with nature, and creating/hosting events in service of mine and my clients' personal growth and leadership development.

Website: www.msmcoaching.com

"What I dare to dream for our future is a world made entirely from love."

Melissa Molinero

New Jersey, United States

CHAPTER 24

Begin with Love

MICHELE KEAN

Mid-March loomed a heavy collective fear hard to overcome. It was so massive and would have been easy to succumb to. Gratefully, I realized, I could not make rational decisions or discernments coming from a frenetic place. So I began to dig, not outside of me, but within.

My inner landscape, through years of practice, typically is a soothing place where I find guidance and truth. This time it was shaken and I kept being pulled with seemingly little escape from the overload of outside information. I turned inward again, and again, surrendering to any calm I could find.

Had this been an answer to combined prayers, perhaps even the prayers of ancestors? A global pause and re-connection to realize our importance, power and potential?

Of course, we did not pray many would experience a horrific illness or die from a pandemic that stretched beyond borders across the planet in a blink of an eye, affecting billions in countless ways while mourning loss, out-of-work or overworked, feeling confused, lied to, fearing for our lives and the future. Of course we did not pray for these specifics. However, we had prayed for the chance for change; a chance to rise from complacency. Whether we welcome it or fight it, is up to us.

It was not a singular person asking, but a global mass, longing to find purpose and the joys of life, to work less, laugh more, heal the earth, share their passions, rise out from the rat race, and start anew.

Things didn't go wrong, they already were. The pause is almost a requirement to tap back into what had been forgotten. It was not being done in the busy-ness of business, in the frenzy of fear, in the angst of anxiety. No amount of vacations would heal it. A jolt was needed. The entire world to be affected, in fact had to be infected, in order to take note.

Solving global relationships is most beneficial once one's own relationships are healed and thriving, most importantly the relationship to self. Enter in Social Distancing, which felt to me more of Personal Connecting. It allowed space for all parts of us to heal, including the auric body which is approximately three feet. In a social distance of six feet we are given the freedom of each individual's physical, emotional, mental, and spiritual bodies. We finally were giving and getting the space we desire and deserve. I became inspired and excited to elevate from what had become normal, but as always, I had to begin at the ground level.

I do feel prepared for this era for the foundation of my childhood was based on an unsteady accumulation of generations of secrets. An authority figure in our family's life was unable to wake up from this and thus continued to lay down more lies. Any truth was ignored or suppressed. Every emotion was judged and ridiculed. As a young child I innocently gave away my power.

Looking back, I had one constant saving grace in my corner, and that was my mother. I struggled to express any appreciation for her at the time because it was so hard to even love myself. I may not have been able to come to this conclusion unless I had a steadfast stream of conscious self-healing, but it would take many years.

Later in life, I finally saw how we were taught to judge, blame, and condemn not only others but ourselves. We were deluded to believe we were divided and unworthy of love. The beautiful truth was we were not divided, no matter how much it felt to be so and we were worthy of all love that outlasts infinity. Once I could see the game, I could decide not to play and begin to rebuild. It is an ever-working art and I still find myself back in the muck, feeling weak and isolated.

Lost in the ruse, we lose our own self. However, opposition will exist only as long as we allow there to be opposition. Some are open and ready for the truth while others resist it, complain, blame, and fight. Each journey is as unique as the individual.

When we trust in conditioning and belief systems, we are not living in truth. The beliefs we have been taught are already untrue. The beliefs we instill, knowingly or unknowingly, in others are also not coming from truth. You know the beliefs: "I'm not good enough." "The universe hates me." "I'm not worthy of love." The list goes on and on and on! It's an old system of sick and tired beliefs. When we get sick and tired of the sick and tired, we can then change.

There are layers put in place from childhood from those that were doing the best they knew, even if it seemed the worst. Their worst was their best. The more cleared, the closer we can get to the inner guidance connected with us, our Soul gets excited that we can hear more clearly. Our True Self which has never left us, can shine!

One can stray far from instincts and intuition. It is stifled, silenced, disowned and life is lived inauthentically. Living in falsehood, there is little truth and vast confusion. Similarly, when we attempt to live by someone else's truth, it also is quite a mess.

Like countless others, I survived a scary system and I grew up. Though I was not unscathed, for I had unhealthy tendencies, heading toward narcissism. In my favor, I became curious to know who I didn't want to be then took deeper dives into the falsities I was trained in. It took dedication and consistency along with compassion for myself to begin the unraveling. My true nature began to emerge which was actually quite lovable and joyful!

The True Self has room to expand when we give attention to the areas calling to be cleared of dirty debris. We feel lighter and one step closer to liberation. I had to first question the firmly anchored false systems and come clean as to where I was not living as authentically as possible. Being ready is a pivotal piece of the puzzle, wherever I felt resistance, I could tell there was just way more work to do!

There are many that don't wish to do inner work and it cannot be forced upon anyone. In fact, forcing it upon our own self, simply causes more resistance! Now, let's consider a bunch of people who have not done inner work and they put a bunch more people in power that have not done so either. I'm sure you can see what that looks like.

We are told those in higher positions lay foundations of lies. Or perhaps these are lies too. Bottom line is the limiting beliefs and reinforced conditioning were all lies already. The only truth resides inside each of us. Resistance will appear when we go against the wisdom of the heart and direct intuition. Try to accept something you don't believe in deep down, it is like an untruth of your Soul. This is all taught, by many, to be ignored, swallowed or set aside. This shutdown gave way to be still, understand this resistance, be with emotions, look within and uncover. To meet the rawness and be with it completely and authentically.

Some of us see an unhealthy assortment of systems and structures currently in place where we are judged and ridiculed if we believe in this and not that. We are judged, even ridiculed if we believe in this and not that. It doesn't even matter what it is, someone will criticize it. Much of what we are taught was taught by others based on their unhealthy conditioning, patterns and beliefs. I am grateful to have been curious to want to break the cycle. As difficult as it is.

The slowing down across the globe, gave a chance to rid these old stories once and for all to step into a more stable, joyful life. We didn't need the virus, but we did need something to show us we are more than whom we have become. An outside force will not solve woes yet it can be the catalyst to see more clearly.

Most are never shown how to hone intuition, let alone acknowledge it. Taught and conditioned by another who was taught and conditioned. There is a great devastation, a disservice to humankind of teaching someone a lie to make them believe it as true. Whether the teacher understood it as a lie or not.

Why are we afraid to check in with our own guidance? Yes, we have been taught not to. Who cares! It is time to re-teach and re-create. It's time for a re-do. Get curious and connect to this mystery!

When centered in compassion, unbiased, united, limitless Love of who you are, life is beyond pleasurable. Out of alignment and acting against the heart's desires, life is a muck of confusion.

Many years, working on transmuting my past still I often felt complacent and stagnant. I was ready to step into my power but I wasn't doing so. I kept getting stuck in the busy-ness I so hated. I would rush through tasks fed up with the over-stimulated, distracted, highly reactive, stressful and addictive nature of the "normal" all around me. I knew I was more yet I wasn't doing anything about it.

When we slow down we can sense what is in our hearts, we know what is real and what is not. We are more apt to make deliberate and conscious decisions. I believed in all my heart this was a deluxe time to get back to basics and re-evaluate my life. Yet I still wasn't practicing what I was preaching! So, on June 1st, I got a hefty dose of my own medicine.

On that day, I had been pushing against the calm, efforting a lunge to reestablish a state of normalcy. I knew I was not ready. I was content in the silence, even as an extrovert. Though I didn't want to go back to the old system, it was all I knew. I spent an entire day with interviews, writings, calendars, and to-do lists. As a reward, I went for a hike with my husband. I had made the strides to re-enter a stable future and then I got totally flat out.

It was a hazardous part of the path, where most of the crafted boardwalk lay under an area of swamp, mud, and muck! We had been walking this almost daily and I had become cocky, not deliberate with my steps. Then I broke my ankle. Stuck in the mud and muck, I was completely unable to use my right foot and went into shock. My husband carried me as far as he could. I wailed in agony the entire few yards. A team of first responders would have to carry me the rest of the couple more hundred yards.

Grounded for the next several weeks, I steeped in a mix of great agony, pity parties, and emotional spikes plus immense surrender, healing and awe. I focused on gratitude. I told my body, including the broken parts, how much I loved and appreciated them. There was not a moment where I angered at my body but instead, loved myself even more than before. I even revelled in the immense change from childhood where I was shameful and self-loathing.

When I was squirming the most in pain, I reached to the wisdom of friends to remind me to be present. Meditating multiple times a day, I could be with the pain and discomfort. I allowed all of it and sometimes even rose above it.

I became clear of my basic needs and got better at expressing them. More fragments of old belief systems that keep me small and disempowered fell away. Fossils of anxiety that kept me distracted and asleep became unearthed.

In a fast pace, I become highly stressed, tending to irrationally develop decisions, lost in a reactive mode. Slowing down makes me stop long enough to notice those reactions and choose differently. Focusing on what is important as I have time to feel it through. In my healing, I became excited to be more methodical and do things on purpose with purpose.

I was even grateful that my injury happened in nature. As I sat in the mud, shivering in the wet clothes, crying in pain, I couldn't help but feel the closest I've ever felt to Earth. No evidence is necessary to observe the planet is also in peril. It only took humans to stop for a moment, for the airways to unclog and animals to feel safe again to move and live. Coming home and healing ourselves, the Earth, too, could heal. The synchronicity is beyond amazing.

I know of no other event in history that has affected all of us on a global level in a short period of time. It is all-inclusive with no segregation because anyone can have an impaired immune system. There have been many other devastations and crises but it didn't affect all of us so quickly at relatively the same time. We had to be shaken a little more to pay attention. Deeply asleep in complacency, we were given a jolt to propel us and possibly free us.

So, let's do it! Let's stop this cycle. But let's do it together. Let's take that scary step off the wheel. It is our nature to come together, for we are not divided.

Tune to truth. See what is available from the inside. Rediscover, unlock. Stop the search outside. Find truth not from a scripture, a book or a bible, one authority, one teacher, one master, one guru, and not from any other, but in and of our own inner self! Once we come home to ourselves we will be present to come home to each other.

Many were in search of a better everything. The systems and structures are sick, tired, broken down, and not working. Let us not bypass the synchrony of those words. We too had to get sick, because we are so tired. We needed it all to break down, to stop and to NOT work. And what happens then? You re-build! You clear the debris and the clutter and you move on! If you do not create a constructive, collaborative, more evolved system, it will surely decay once more. Let us build anew, beyond the old and broken, sick and perished. Beyond our imaginations!

This Great Pause supported me to let go of old out-dated debris. And I came back home to what I had learned. What we all have in common. LOVE.

About Michele

Michele has a unique sense of humor and a laugh that can brighten (almost) anybody's day. An advocate for holistic self-care and living your most authentic self, she is a Justice of the Peace, author of the upcoming children's book "Rio & Silas with Love," Reiki Master, and Licensed Massage Therapist.

Originally from South Jersey, she moved to Connecticut because she could, and has created a safe haven there. A turbulent past taught her to embrace every moment and to love more than ever before. Michele learned that to accept is to truly let go. She trusts her body's wisdom and natural healing. Michele's purpose and passion shines and thrives as she does Marriage and Blessing Ceremonies, Guided Meditations and Healings on all levels. She loves yoga and practices mindfulness. Nature is her sanctuary.

Despite her human appearance she may, in fact, be a butterfly.

"When centered in compassion, unbiased, united, limitless Love of who you are, life is beyond pleasurable."

Michele Kean

Connecticut, United States

CHAPTER 25

Embrace

ELIZABETH B. HILL, MSW

In the "before times" (aka mid-March 2020) I went on a date. We met on a beach, since restaurants, bars, and coffee shops had just been closed the day before. People were talking about this new six-foot rule but that seemed such silly business at the time. This man and I hugged in greeting and sat on a bench at the beach and watched the sunset. It was lovely. Then we went to his apartment and he made me dinner. It was delicious. We had a nice meal and good conversation, but we didn't quite click. When I got home, my mom (who had been staying with my grandma so I could go out) ran out the door to her own house. It would be the last time I'd see her in months.

In the morning, I watched the news with my 96-year-old grandma. My governor condemned me. He spoke about young people needing to stop going out and stay home to protect their grandmas. Now at 41, I'm no spring chicken, but apparently I run around like one. I felt horrible. I felt scared. The guy I'd been on a date with was a doctor-who knows how many patients he had seen and what they had. I might have really put Grandma-and our whole family-in danger.

In truth, I counted the fourteen days until we'd know I wasn't infected. I was a bit sure I'd gotten us all the COVID. Thankfully, I had not. The fourteen days passed and we remained well.

So. I was grounded. Mom had fled the scene, as well she should have. My mom acts like she's about fifteen, but she is seventy-one by the calendar system we've all agreed upon as a society, so she is in the "vulnerable population." We were too scared to have the caregiver come in who usually came in four mornings a week to help with Grandma. Usually my kids are with their dad half the time and with me half the time, but now they were with me full-time. Their dad works at a hospital and he was kind enough to let them stay with us to keep them and all of us safe. He's a very caring father and this was very hard for him to do.

Grandma, Raven, James, and I were in this home together 24-7. My son was overjoyed not to be in school. My daughter was missing her friends terribly. They both missed their dad. They appeared to be doing school-but how would I know? I was on the phone or Zoom coaching my clients, helping Grandma get from place to place, and making seemingly endless meals and snacks (for about a month I baked each day). Plus, there was the time I had to set aside each day to lay down and cry about the end of the world. For real.

I was determined to KEEP IT TOGETHER. I knew WHAT TO DO. I had my social work, yoga, mindfulness, and coach-training under my belt. I knew how to handle this! I was prepared for this! I knew that drinking alcohol would be a downfall for me during this high-stress time, so I stopped drinking entirely. I made an intense hour-by-hour schedule so I could get everything done that needed to get done, including the aforementioned crying over the state of the world. I already worked from home so no problem there. My two clients that I met in person easily switched over to video calls. Easy-peasy-lemon-squeezy. I got this. I am a LEADER! I decided to run a 21-day manifesting experience (why not?), going live with 20-minute meditations for 21 days. I recorded videos, including, "We're Grounded. Here's Why I'm Not Afraid." I had four books in the works of my own, plus those of my clients. I was on top of this.

I WAS GOING TO ROCK THE PANDEMIC. The only thing I didn't think I could handle was not dating and the pleasures that come from that (I'll let you fill in the blanks on whatever that could be). I was not sure how I could manage that.

Wowzers.

Did I have a lot to learn.

I found ways to sort of get my *"needs"* addressed, but what I couldn't replace was the touch, the hugs. My body and heart literally ached for hugs. There was no replacing it.

My kids are thirteen and fourteen and not currently amenable to hugging me. Grandma has always had a six-feet rule, with a clear, unspoken message of, *"Thou shalt not enter my sphere!!!!"* So I was not getting hugs from the people in my house.

About ten weeks in, this became too excruciating and I had to phone a friend. My dear Karla came to visit me. I designated her my hugging friend. She was in the bubble. My mental health was more important than any potential risk at this point. My soul was leaking out my finger-tips from lack of touch. Her hugs picked up my soul and put it back in.

I also found ways to connect with spirit in ways that felt physical. This is hard to explain, but in my meditation, I began to be able to call in a guide and actually feel their presence-this began to present as a feeling of touch on my shoulder blades behind my heart. This was one of the blessings of this time. There were many others. These are a few.

Time with my children. I felt so blessed to have had my kids full-time again after five years of only having them half of the week. Ten whole weeks with my children. Somehow, being in this incubator with two teenagers made us communicate better than we had before.

Intergenerational love. I needed to ask the kids to help more with Grandma and this created some special time between them that is very unique and will be a memory for them and me for years to come. To see my daughter and son help their great grandmother up the stairs, saying sweet words of encouragement to her, filled my heart to the brim.

The sun on our skin. I got much closer to my Grandma and she shared things with me that she'd never shared with me before. We also began to spend time together outside. Grandma had always been a sun-worshipper, but other than a few ventures to doctor visits, she had not been outside for any length of time for years. You read that right. *Years.* She had suffered several falls and for whatever reason had been declining our offers to go outside for a very long time. One day during quarantine, when I said, "Let's go outside today, it's really nice out," she surprised me with an answer of, "Oh, yes, that sounds like a good idea." The kids and I were shocked-and so very happy.

It is now common for the kids and I to sit with Grandma outside in the afternoon, to breathe the fresh air, to see the sun dance on the pool, and to listen to the birds sing. Grandma says the birds have chosen to live in our yard because they like us better than anyone else. Grandma tells me what the birds are saying to us, and this is quite an education, let me tell you.

Appreciation of hugs and intimacy. I know now what a gift and blessing touch is. I will never take these for granted again. I know what it means for someone to go without it. I know what a gift a hug can be for someone who hasn't had one and craves it. I learned I can cope without sex (though I certainly don't want to), but it is extremely bad for my mental health to go without physical touch. I learned my spirit guides can help me take care of my physical needs in real-time.

Spiritual guidance. I got closer to my spirit guides and divine presence than ever before. Rather than a distant thought or something I'd look up to, spirit and the divine became my constant companions. We would talk. When I needed a hug and no human could be there for me, I felt them envelope me and hold me. I knew I was not alone, no matter what. I had them with me, I only had to decide whether I would notice it or not.

Life can be easy. This collaborative writing project has come together with such ease and grace and play. I am truly in the flow of the divine. When we connect with this, our work can be easy.

The power of acceptance. Some days aren't going to be good and there's nothing you can do about it. Some days, no matter how hard I rallied, it didn't matter. Some days you can't rock the pandemic, you gotta let the pandemic rock you. When I finally would accept this and let myself lay down and cry and rest, life felt better, and I could turn around quicker than if I stayed with fighting it.

My garden. Gardening is my heart. I set up two raised beds outside and started a hydroponic Tower Garden in my house. Now I'm eating tomatoes, lettuce, and swiss chard from my garden again and it feels so right.

My chosen family. I have some pretty epic, fairy-tale-esque family by blood, but I also have an incredible support network of loving, spiritual, divinely-provided human beings that I consider family that I got to choose.

I am attracting more and more wise, creative, loving souls each day. I learned that I deserve to be surrounded with people with hearts like mine, who practice what they preach, who live full-on in this messy, magical playscape of a life. I can be myself with them and it feels easy.

Our future, should we dare to dream.

What we used to consider as "normal" was anything but. "Normal" wasn't working for most humans-or for our planet. We get to choose the "normal" we will accept. We all get to decide what things we pick back up. We get to choose what things we will let fall to the past. We get to pick which new ideas and paradigms we will live into. So, what will we choose?

I will choose to continue living a life that feels right to me, whether people understand it or not. I will love those that I love, whether people understand me loving them or not. I will seek unity and connection rather than difference and divisiveness. I will ask for help and let life work well. I will give myself props for ROCKING THE QUARANTINE and also be, like, girl, next pandemic you can TIGER KING THE WHOLE SEASON and it's okay. I will clear out what doesn't feel good, and stick with what does feel good.

I will accept what is happening as what is, in fact, happening, rather than fighting it. I will embrace the moment that is presenting itself to me. Borrowing a theater term, I will say, "Yes, and-" and will keep creating the world I'd love to live in no matter what I'm presented with.

Most of all, I will stay in the wonder and magic of life. I will remember that I do not have all of this figured out. That there is more in this mystery to unfold. That it's not my job to tell anyone else their lessons.

I will continue in the belief that this (and all of life) is happening *for* us, not *to* us. That even the heartbreaking, the frightening, the confusing parts of life, have wisdom and blessings available for me and all of us. We all have our own wisdom and blessings to find, and our own mysteries to solve. This is the universe's divine gift to us. We get to choose whether we meet it with eyes, hands, hearts open, or if we cringe and push away.

I will keep pausing and sitting with whatever is present.

I will keep sharing my story and give others the platform to do the same.

I will let love lead the way.

I will keep *coming home*.

ABOUT ELIZABETH

Elizabeth is CEO and Publisher of Green Heart Living Press. She is the best-selling author of "Love Notes: Daily Wisdom for the Soul" and "Green Your Heart, Green Your World: Avoid Burnout, Save the World and Love Your Life." With over 15 years of experience writing and leading collaborations in the nonprofit sphere, Elizabeth helps clients through the process of writing and publishing their stories. Trained as a social worker, yoga teacher, and life coach, she weaves creativity, spirituality, and mindfulness into her work with clients. Elizabeth lives in a matriarchal palace in Connecticut with her family and the neighborhood bears.

Website: www.greenheartliving.com

"I will let love lead the way...
I will keep coming home."

ELIZABETH B. HILL, MSW

Connecticut, United States

ALSO BY ELIZABETH B. HILL, MSW

Love Notes: Daily Wisdom for the Soul

Green Your Heart, Green Your World:
Avoid Burnout, Save the World and Love Your Life

ABOUT GREEN HEART LIVING PRESS

Our Mission:

Making the World a More Loving and Peaceful Place,
One Book at a Time

The Green Heart Living team guides authors through the process of writing and publishing their personal stories of transformation and growth. Green Heart Living Press authors write to heal, inspire others, and to grow their impact in the world.

Elizabeth B. Hill, MSW, ACC is the founder and CEO of Green Heart Living Press. As a bestselling author, Elizabeth helps clients through the process of writing and publishing their stories and books, as well as utilizing writing to grow their businesses and impact in the world. Elizabeth's special expertise in helping those with anxiety and high-stress lives ensures nothing gets in the way of her clients' writing projects.

Whether your book is in your mind and heart - or already written but waiting to be published - Elizabeth and the Green Heart Living team can help you bring your book out into the world with ease and joy.

www.greenheartlivingpress.com